Praise 1

As a retired pediatric AIDS nurse and longtime peace activist, I approached Susan Hunt Babinski's powerful account of her time as a nurse in Vietnam in the early years of the war with great interest. In spare, direct, and lively prose, the author describes her transformation from a young, inexperienced nurse who was excited to be beginning a compassionate adventure leading to a hard-won realization. "I was not just a healer," Babinski writes. "I was part of the United States Army. Some of us worked in the fields, some in the jungle, some in airplanes, and some in hospitals. We were all part of the war machine. Me too. I was a part of 'we.'"

In Just a Year: Coming of Age in Vietnam is a compelling, honest story that holds many lessons for a world that still sends young men and women off to die in wars, and too often ignores the contributions of the nurses who bind their wounds and the toll that it takes on them.

    Elena Schwolsky, RN, MPH
    Author of *Waking in Havana: A Memoir of AIDS and Healing in Cuba*

~

Like most nurses who served in Vietnam, Susan Hunt Babinski came back a changed person. Her recollections of this experience remind us of the horror of war, the resiliency of the human spirit, and the debt America still owes such heroes. *In Just a Year* is not a feel-good book, nor could it possibly be. It is, however, an honest book, a courageous book, a book full of heart, and if you look closely, hope. It honors Babinski's life and the lives of other nurses like her who gave so much for so little in return.

Bob Welch
Co-author with Diane Carlson Evans of *Healing Wounds: A Vietnam War Combat Nurse's 10-Year Fight to Win Women a Place of Honor in Washington, D.C.*

~

Susan Hunt was a twenty-two-year-old nurse when she was thrust into a dirty, bloody war 8,000 miles from home. She treated all those in need in Vietnam—Americans and Vietnamese alike—and was witness to the brutality of American soldiers who committed atrocities and felt guilt for the rest of their lives. Nurses fought a different kind of war in Vietnam—one that robbed them of their feelings and sent them home as invisible veterans who had given so much of themselves to the wounded and dying.

I got to know Susan Hunt Babinski as I read this book. She was a nurse who cared for and loved her patients—all of them. She knew war was pain and devastation and did her best to care for its wounded. Like Susan, I was a nurse who knew the war was wrong and did my best to stop it. After the war ended, we walked similar paths—she, caring for traumatized children in the South Bronx and I, in the New York

City public hospital system, caring for others in need. We learned to put our feelings aside in the moment, but the memories were ingrained. We could have worked together to heal the wounds of war, to help former enemies reconcile for peace. I am so sorry we never met.

   Susan M. Schnall, RN
   President, Veterans for Peace Board of Directors
   Co-coordinator, Vietnam Agent Orange Relief and Responsibility Campaign

~

Susan Hunt Babinski has written a compelling memoir of her experiences as an army nurse at the 91st Evacuation Hospital in Vietnam. She describes in detail what happens to soldiers and civilians in war, and while in many ways gruesome, the details are essential. Dr. Babinski went to the 91st Evac when she was 22 years old, straight out of nursing school. She was in no way prepared for what she saw. She, like so many nurses, believed she was supposed to be there for the patients. As all nurses eventually figure out, the medical establishment, and the armed forces in particular, have another agenda. Dr. Babinski's clear recall of many situations rings true for us, nurses who have spent a lifetime in the profession.

After her time in Vietnam, she came home to what many army nurses and soldiers endured. The war was unpopular. People were unfiltered in their condemnation of those who went. Many in the army and many civilians ignored and dismissed them; their physical and emotional wounds were treated in the most horribly cavalier manner. In addition to all that, many people at the 91st Evac Hospital were exposed to Agent Orange, which resulted in a cancer diagnosis for Dr. Babinski and many others. Sadly, she did not survive to see this book to publication.

What Dr. Babinski accomplished after the war was as riveting as her description of war wounds or the sick and injured children she nursed. She pursued a graduate education and specialized in child and adolescent psychiatric nursing. Her work in this area must have been life changing for many of her patients and their families. In her advocacy for the Vietnam Women's Memorial, she helped make sure the nurses who served in Vietnam were recognized in the same way the soldiers were recognized, in a very real and physical way, near the Vietnam Veterans Memorial in Washington, DC. She did observational research to describe other nurses' experiences in Vietnam. After all that, a young English professor dismissed her service during a diatribe about all the "crazy vets" she had in her classes. When Dr. Babinski revealed she was a Vietnam vet, the woman said, "Oh, that doesn't count. You're not really a vet." Once again, nursing was dismissed as unimportant. How many of us have heard that phrase, "Oh, you're just a nurse"?

This book is essential reading for anyone who is interested in what nursing was like during war time. It joins the voices of other nurses (such as Lynda Van Devanter in *Home Before Morning: The Story of an Army Nurse in Vietnam*, Ellen Emerson White in *The

Road Home, and Winnie Smith in *American Daughter Gone to War: On the Front Lines with an Army Nurse in Vietnam*) who shared their experiences as nurses in Vietnam. It is also essential for other nurses to read so they know they are not alone in the experience of being young and exposed to horror, loss, and grief; and perhaps more importantly, how to craft a useful and fulfilling life with those experiences.

Valery Hughes, RN, FNP-BC
Ellen Matzer, RN
Authors of *Nurses on the Inside: Stories of the HIV/AIDS Epidemic in NYC* and *Beyond the Mask*

~

Susan Hunt Babinski's book, *In Just a Year*, is a remarkable account of her year as a US Army nurse in Vietnam during the American war there. Her experiences—from the many American servicemen and officers who passed through her life in that terrible time, to the wounded Vietnamese children that she cared for, to the discovery of war crimes committed by American troops and the realization that "We," all of us, were part of the war machine committing these horrors—this is the war as it really was. Romantic encounters and children made orphans, horrible suffering and beautiful sunrises, it's all there. Yes, women, too, went to war, and came home forever changed.

Michael Wong
National Vice President, Veterans for Peace
Co-founder, Pivot to Peace

~

Susan's story is one of love, stark terror, courage, and commitment. Young and adventuresome, Susan, sworn in as a second lieutenant one year after graduating as a nurse, volunteered for assignment to Vietnam in 1967. Between the exhilarating rush of caring for severely injured children and battle-wounded soldiers, Susan details enduring trauma to her private life, swept in a rapid transition from nurse to miliary personnel. With simple, straightforward descriptions of her nursing experiences, Susan immerses readers into the unpatterned, frightening work of an evacuation hospital. Her descriptions of injured, orphaned children offer insight into this rarely recognized consequence of war. Forever changed by her year in Vietnam, she returns home wanting to be seen, to be acknowledged for her contributions, to be thanked by a country dismissive of the conflict. Susan has poignantly documented both the horror of war and the life-changing impact of war on those who choose to stand up for their country.

Frances Ward, PhD, RN, NP
Professor Emerita, David R. Devereaux Chair of Nursing, Temple University
Author of *The Door of Last Resort: Memoirs of a Nurse Practitioner*

IN JUST A YEAR

Coming of Age in Vietnam

Susan Hunt Babinski

Purple Breeze Press

Copyright © 2023 Estate of Susan Hunt Babinski

Purple Breeze Press, LLC

purplebreezepress.com

In Just a Year: Coming of Age in Vietnam is a memoir. It reflects the author's recollections of experiences over time. Some names and descriptions have been changed. Some events have been drawn from memory. Some dialogue has been recreated or reimagined.

Except in the case of brief quotations used in articles and reviews, no part of this book may be reproduced, stored in a retrieval system, or transmitted in any form without the author's permission.

Library of Congress Cataloguing in Publication Data
Names: Babinski, Susan Hunt, author
Title: In Just a Year: Coming of Age in Vietnam
Description: First edition. | Purple Breeze Press, 2023
Library of Congress Control Number: 2023903077
ISBN Paperback: 9798385532148

All personal photos are from the author.

Photo of Vietnam Women's Memorial from National Park Service. No protection is claimed in original U.S. Government works.

The Four Loves by CS Lewis © 1960 CS Lewis Pte Ltd Extract used with permission.

Manuscript edited by Hubert F. Babinski and Rebecca Williams Mlynarczyk.

Book designed and copyedited by Meg Vezzu / megvezzu.com.

For our son,

Andrzej Babinski

CONTENTS

Introduction by Rebecca Williams Mlynarczyk	1
Joining the Army Nurse Corps	17
Sandy Beaches, Pumpkin, and Ronald Colman	29
Pediatric Nursing	43
Daily Life	67
Adventures with Charlie	85
Sunrise and Censure	91
Enemies	99
Doing and Dying	109
Outside of Heaven	117
There and Here	137
My Return to the World	155
Monuments and Memories	169
Acknowledgments by Hubert F. Babinski	179

Introduction

Rebecca Williams Mlynarczyk

I MET SUSAN HUNT BABINSKI in 1990, when we were students in the same graduate class at New York University. Our professor, Margot Ely, encouraged us to form small writing support groups to see us through the doctoral process. Three of us—Jane Isenberg, Pat Juell, and I—knew each other from previous classes in our English education program. We needed a fourth member to round out the group. Like us, Susan was a nontraditional student— a white woman in her forties, married, and with a successful career but wanting something more as she approached midlife. We decided to go back to school and get our PhDs. Susan had a nursing background and was studying psychology. Perfect, we thought. With three English majors, we need a nurse/therapist to pull us back from the brink when things get rocky. It turned out to be a winning combination. While working on our dissertations and for nearly thirty years after that, we met monthly, finding a vacant classroom at NYU and sitting around a table to share our writing.

During many of these Friday night sessions, Susan, speaking in her soft, soothing nurse's voice, sometimes barely more than a whisper, talked about her year as a young nurse in Vietnam from 1967 to 1968. First, she worked on a pediatric ward, taking care of Vietnamese children with war injuries and birth defects, and then, after the Tet Offensive began in January, on a PreOp/PostOp unit tending to the wounded soldiers and civilians who poured into the 91st Evacuation Hospital in Tuy Hòa. Fresh out of the Rhode Island School of Nursing in 1966, she had enlisted in the army. After basic training in Texas, she was sworn in as a second lieutenant and headed to her first assignment, working on the pediatric ward of Fitzsimons Army Medical Center in Denver. Then, in the spring of 1967, she and her friend Joan volunteered for a one-year tour of duty in Vietnam. She was twenty-two years old.

Over the years, as Susan shared her writing with Jane, Pat, and me, she taught us what it was like to experience the horrors of war while also feeling the thrill of living in the moment as life and death hung in the balance. Like so many other nurses who had served in that war, Susan quoted Charles Dickens when reflecting on her year in Vietnam: "It was the best of times, it was the worst of times."

In the early group meetings, we focused on researching and writing our dissertations, the much-dreaded exit requirement for the PhD. Susan knew from the start that she wanted to focus on the experiences of other women nurses who served in Vietnam. Through her professional connections, she recruited a small group of women who were willing to participate in a series of in-depth interviews reflecting on their experiences during the war and after returning home. In those pre-Zoom days, this meant that Susan had to drive all over the East Coast to meet with the women in person, talking with them for hours, and then painstakingly transcribing every word of their audiotaped conversations.

During our small-group meetings, Susan would read aloud from the interview transcripts. Working together, we searched for common themes expressed by the nurses, such as recurring nightmares or trouble forming close relationships. We were also on the lookout for an observation unique to just one of the nurses, known in qualitative research as an outlier. The women she interviewed were high achievers, pursuing additional degrees after returning from Vietnam, often rising to the top of their chosen professions. Most found they couldn't settle into a routine nine-to-five job after returning from Vietnam. They still craved the adrenaline-fueled excitement they felt while working in a war zone. Some chose to remain in the military. Those who stayed in nursing often opted to work in the operating room or emergency room, once again dealing with matters of life and death.

Veterans of all wars have been reticent in sharing their wartime experiences, sometimes waiting decades to talk about them with anyone, often dying with the stories untold. Talking about the war was especially fraught for Vietnam veterans, who returned home to be booed and spat upon by anti-war protesters. Susan's nurse participants felt free to open up to her about their experiences, knowing that as a Vietnam veteran herself, she would truly understand.

The women veterans who volunteered for Susan's study were also hoping that this research would focus attention on the importance of women's contributions during the war. Women who served in Vietnam often referred to themselves as the invisible vets. Thankfully, very few of them died in the war, yet even the living can become invisible. Only eight women are listed among the dead on the Vietnam Veterans Memorial Wall, dedicated in 1982. Two years later, a statue called The Three Soldiers, honoring the men who served, was installed near the Wall. Aside from the dead, women were simply not there. Seeing this invisibility, Diane Carlson Evans, whose tour of duty as an army nurse was just a year after Susan's, led a nine-year struggle to get approval and funding for a statue honoring the women who served in Vietnam. Finally, on November 11, 1993, the Vietnam Women's Memorial statue was dedicated. It stands just fifty-nine feet from the Memorial Wall. This was the first monument ever to acknowledge the contributions of American women who served abroad in wartime.

Susan went to Washington, DC, for the dedication, which inspired the title of her dissertation: "Did We Have to Wait Twenty-Five Years to Weep in Front of a Monument? A Qualitative Study of Six Women Vietnam Veteran Nurses" (available from New York University ProQuest Dissertations Publishing, Publication No. 9701473). Jane, Pat, and I attended Susan's dissertation defense in 1996. The committee members and outside readers were impressed by Susan's research and approved the dissertation unanimously. But they had one big question for Susan:

"Where are you in all of this? We want to hear your story."

Susan spent the rest of her life trying to answer this question.

~

The writing group continued to meet as we turned to other projects. Jane wrote and published a series of murder mysteries. Pat brought us her poems. I worked on books and articles related to my work teaching writing to multilingual students at the City University of New York. And Susan wrote about Vietnam.

Often her writings were short and fragmentary, perhaps jotted on the back of an envelope or in a little notebook she happened to grab when a new idea struck. It was hard for Susan to find time for writing. Her job as a psychologist at the Bronx Children's Psychiatric Center was intense and exhausting. She chose to work with children who were placed in the day care program rather than being hospitalized because she felt it was important for children to be kept at home with their families if at all possible. She spent her days driving around the South Bronx, a dangerous neighborhood at the time, making home visits to families in trouble. She loved this work and felt she was making a difference. In some ways it was a continuation of her work on the pediatric ward in Vietnam, helping vulnerable children in the midst of a violent and chaotic world.

When she got home from work, she had lots to do in her other roles as wife and mother. She had married Hubert Babinski in 1970, two years after returning from Vietnam, and they had a son, Andrzej. Susan and Hugh had a large and devoted circle of friends, with whom they often went to plays, operas, and art exhibits in New York City. They also attended and hosted elaborate dinner parties. With such an active work schedule and social life, there was not much time left over for writing.

After twenty-eight years working full time for the Bronx Children's Psychiatric Center, Susan retired, feeling she would like to have a less demanding schedule with more time for writing. But soon after her supposed retirement, she accepted a part-time job at the Isabella Center for Rehabilitation and Nursing Care in upper Manhattan, serving as a psychologist for fragile, mostly elderly patients. As it turned out, she didn't have as much free time as she had expected. There were multiple forms to fill out and so many residents who needed someone to listen to their life stories or gently help them find their way back to their room when they got lost. Dr. B, as she was known there, soon became an essential worker at Isabella.

Still, when our Friday evening writing group meeting rolled around, Susan was always there and usually managed to bring something to share. We did not send our writings to group members in advance. Instead, we brought what we had to the group and read it aloud. We never rushed our discussions, giving everyone a chance to respond in depth. As Pat once said, "We give ourselves the gift of time." And Susan did take her time, writing bits and pieces of her Vietnam story over many years.

Shortly after she was awarded the PhD in 1996, Susan began to bring short writings that gave us a glimpse of her experiences in Vietnam. She might read the story of Johnny, a sweet young soldier who won multiple Purple Hearts for his injuries. Or she might describe one of her boyfriends. There were a series of them, including Jerry, the special one. And then there were the children Susan cared for—Chubby Bunny, Kim, Jimmy/Jo, and many others. Working on the pediatric ward would not have been the same without Charlie, the corpsman who loved the kids as much as Susan did and worked alongside her to keep them safe and provide a measure of comfort.

Susan has a distinctive voice as a writer—simple and direct, going straight to the heart, the same way she looks out at the reader from the photograph on the cover of this book. As Susan read aloud the heart-wrenching stories of her experiences in Vietnam, Jane earned the nickname DC (Designated Crier). She openly wept while Pat and I, more reserved group members, often found ourselves wiping away tears. Susan never cried. She just kept reading in her soft, calm voice.

It was in this same voice that Susan often told us how much she appreciated the chance to share these stories with the three of us. She hadn't spoken often about her experiences in Vietnam, even to her husband. Like other veterans, she was hesitant to talk about the war and was conflicted about whether to make her experiences public. There were issues of confidentiality—what she was revealing about herself and about others—as well as doubts about whether outsiders would truly understand. It took years before she felt able to share her stories in a public setting, but the few times she did, the responses were overwhelmingly positive, with audience members coming up afterward to share their own stories.

Gradually, Susan became convinced that it was important for everyone to understand what women veterans had contributed in Vietnam. When she arrived there in 1967, she thought of herself as a nurse, not a member of the military. Her view of her role changed completely when she learned, midway through the year, that the US Army had killed the parents of one of her young South Vietnamese patients and destroyed their entire village. Susan could no longer think of herself as just a nurse and not part of the larger system.

When she returned to the States, she certainly didn't regard herself as a hero, but she did feel her work there had made a difference and should be recognized. When she learned that there would be a ceremony commemorating the twentieth anniversary of the Vietnam Women's Memorial statue on the National Mall in Washington, Susan volunteered to be one of the speakers. She workshopped the speech with Pat and me (by this time, Jane had relocated to the Seattle area). Her bravery as she stood at an outdoor podium delivering that speech on November 11, 2013, was palpable. The nurses and other veterans in the audience were captivated. (A video of Susan delivering that speech is available online: http://www.vietnamwomensmemorial.org/videos/susan-hunt-babinski.html.) In 2015, she published a condensed version of the speech, entitled "Yellow Flowers," in Volume 8 of *The Westchester Review*.

Susan was never completely comfortable talking about Vietnam in public, but by 2015 she was determined to push her doubts aside and publish a memoir based on her experiences as a young nurse. She even had the title: *In Just a Year*.

~

In the spring of 2016, Pat and I received an email from Susan. She was very sorry, but she wouldn't be able to make our Friday evening writing group. She had been feeling ill and was having a series of medical tests. A few days later, she received the diagnosis: she was suffering from late-stage ovarian cancer. There were treatments to make her more comfortable and extend her life a bit, but she was a nurse and she understood what the doctors were saying. This was a terminal diagnosis.

It wasn't long before we scheduled another group meeting. This time we decided it would be better if

Pat and I took the train up to Westchester to meet in Susan and Hugh's condo. Hugh loves to cook and to eat. He volunteered to make lunch.

Susan's bravery as she faced her own death was equal to her bravery in Vietnam. Perhaps they were related. She never complained or expressed anger about her condition. The only traces of anger related to her knowledge that she and so many others had been exposed to Agent Orange while serving in Vietnam. In 1993, while she was attending the dedication of the Women's Memorial, she learned for the first time that the 91st Evacuation Hospital, where she had served, had been declared an Agent Orange Center. Everyone who worked there had been exposed, and many had subsequently died of various types of cancer.

Susan realized it was too late to do anything about that. What she could do, and what she was determined to do, was to finish her Vietnam memoir. She now approached this project with an urgency and intensity we had never seen before.

Looking back at my email records from 2016 through 2018, I'm surprised to see how often Pat and I took the train to Westchester to consult about Susan's writing. We would sit in her living room and listen as she read her latest draft aloud while Hugh puttered around in the kitchen, making lunch. Sometimes we feared she was too weak to read the writing herself, but she always pushed through her exhaustion. She wanted to hear her story in her own voice.

By the late spring of 2018, she was too ill to continue writing. She died at home on July 14. She was seventy-three years old.

~

Although Susan and Hugh had a wonderful, close marriage, he had never read her writings about Vietnam, not even her dissertation. In her gentle way, she made it clear this was her story, not his. But he knew how much this writing meant to her and how dedicated she had been, especially after her diagnosis, to publishing it as a book.

As he grieved, he immersed himself in all the drafts, trying to see the whole picture. He was well qualified to do this work, holding a PhD in comparative literature from Columbia University. In February 2019, he reached out to Pat and me, asking if we'd be willing to meet with him to talk about how to shape and edit Susan's writings about Vietnam. We had a number of meetings, and Hugh kept working on the manuscript. These meetings continued until

January 2020, and then the COVID-19 pandemic hit. Meetings were no longer a possibility.

During the months of isolation, as Hugh read and reread Susan's writings, he realized for the first time just how deeply her life had been shaped by her time in Vietnam. He had been too sad and exhausted when she died to hold any kind of memorial service. Almost three years later, after learning what Susan's military service in Vietnam had meant to her, he decided that Arlington National Cemetery would be an appropriate resting place for her ashes. He arranged for a full military service. My husband and I were among the many friends and relatives who gathered there to honor Susan on May 14, 2021.

In January 2023, Hugh submitted his most recent edit of Susan's story to the editors of Purple Breeze Press, Frances Ward and Norbert Elliot. A few days later, he signed a contract with them to publish Susan's book. Because I was so familiar with Susan's writing about Vietnam, Fran and Norbert asked me to serve as a developmental editor. Reading through the manuscript, I was impressed with the way Hugh had organized the material into distinct chapters, but I sometimes recalled other versions of the same story. Reviewing additional sources, including an earlier draft, the speech Susan gave at the Women's Memorial in 2013, and the essay she published in 2015, I updated some of the stories with additional details or more colorful language, all in Susan's distinctive voice.

As I read and reread the book, I kept thinking about a time many years ago during one of our writing group meetings at NYU. Susan apologized profusely for not having brought any writing. She had been so busy—work, social events, helping her son with his schoolwork. Then she unzipped her purse, removed her wallet, and took out a crumpled piece of paper with some words typed on it. She explained that this was a quotation from C. S. Lewis's book *The Four Loves*. A young officer had shared it with her in Vietnam one day while he was making the rounds of the unit. This was at a time when Susan was questioning herself. She wondered if she was shutting down her feelings in order to survive the nightmares happening all around her. Lewis writes, "To love at all is to be vulnerable. Love anything, and your heart will certainly be wrung and possibly broken." The only way to escape the pain of existence, he says, is to lock up your heart in "the casket or coffin of your selfishness." Susan understood what Lewis meant. She kept that quotation in her wallet until the day she died as a reminder that if she tried to stay safe and close herself off from feeling, she would no longer be able to love.

Susan returned from Vietnam forever changed. She would never again be the happy-go-lucky party girl who had boarded an army plane to Saigon in the summer of 1967. She had absorbed the trauma of that brutal war. But rather than hating and fearing, she returned home with a deepened understanding of what it means to care for others. She had grown in her ability to accept everyone she met just as they were—young or old, sick or well, military or civilian, American or Vietnamese. Susan never spoke about any of this, but everyone who met her sensed that it was so without a word being said. Now, through the writing she left behind, readers will get to know her as well—the girl who became a woman in just a year.

Brooklyn, New York
February 15, 2023

Joining the Army Nurse Corps

AFTER GRADUATING from Pilgrim High School in Warwick, Rhode Island, in 1963, I attended the Rhode Island Hospital School of Nursing. That was the usual way women, and a few men, became registered nurses then. Career choices for women in my white, middle-class world were limited to nursing, teaching, or secretarial work. Nursing was right for me. I loved caring for people. But I wanted to get married eventually and have children. Nursing sounded exciting and rewarding and good preparation for a future mother.

Of course, a Catholic girl like me could always become a nun, but I never seriously considered that option. Growing up, I remember reading with horror and sadness the Catholic missionary brochures that came to our home. They spoke of the impact of wars and famines in faraway places. Looking at photos of sad-looking, malnourished children—some of them orphans, some born with cleft palates or other birth defects, and some with wartime injuries—made me want to help. In high school, I had read Albert Schweitzer's autobiography, *Out of My Life and Thought*. After reading that book, I had fantasies of being a heroine, doing good work like Dr. Schweitzer. When I volunteered to go to Vietnam, I still had those fantasies.

In the spring of 1965, my second year at the Rhode Island Hospital School of Nursing, a young, handsome US Army recruiter came to speak to us at an assembly. We learned that we could enlist in the army with a student nurse friend in our senior year and have our nursing school tuition paid for while receiving a monthly stipend. After graduating and passing the state boards/registered nurse licensing exams, we would be sent to officers' basic training in San Antonio, Texas. There we would be sworn in as second lieutenants and choose our first billets. That sounded exciting. Joan, one of my classmates and a dear friend, talked about what an adventure it would be, and we decided to join under the "buddy program" as some of our classmates did. We thought of ourselves as nurses, helpers, caregivers. Although it was only a possibility that we would go to Vietnam, that too sounded intriguing. Joining the army seemed like an adventure and much more interesting than marrying my hometown boyfriend. I told him my plan, and we agreed to stay in touch and date again when I returned home from my two-year commitment. In the meantime, we were free to date others.

When Joan and I told our parents that we wanted to join the army, they were horrified. Both sets of parents said, "Absolutely not!" They were determined not to let us sign up. Our fathers had served in the US Army during World War II and had been in battle, but neither ever spoke about it. When Joan's mother was out of town, she convinced her father to sign the consent form. Her mother was furious when she found out.

My mother didn't say too much, but my father was determined not to allow me to enlist. He even hired a lawyer to prevent it. The lawyer pointed out that in my senior year, when I would turn twenty-one, my father no longer had that authority over me. After more discussion, the lawyer drew up a contract for the army to sign that stated I could not be transferred outside the United States before I passed my registered nurse exam and was legally an adult at twenty-one. That made me angry because I was sure the army officials wouldn't sign such a document. But they did.

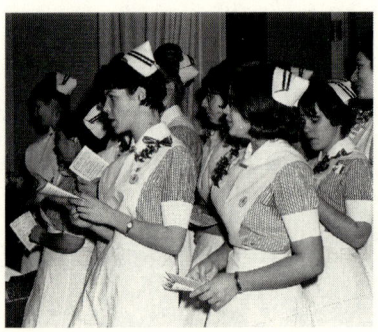

At the beginning of our senior year in nursing school, Joan, I, and a few other nurses were inducted into the army as privates. I bought a bright yellow Vespa scooter with my monthly allowance and had fun driving it around town. My new boyfriend, Joe, had *Susan* painted in large black script across the front.

Basic Training and Fitzsimons Army Medical Center

After graduating from nursing school and passing our licensing exams, Joan, who bought a car, and another nursing school friend of ours, Astrid, drove south to Fort Sam Houston in San Antonio, Texas, for basic training. Astrid's family was Mexican. Her father was a well-known, well-liked medical doctor in their New England community. Like my dad, Astrid's father did not want her to join the army. We asked another classmate, Sylvia, to join us on the drive down. She was adamant in saying "No!" If she came along with us, she was sure we would all be killed. She was African American, and in the mid-1960s, it was not safe for mixed racial groups to travel together in the South.

I was shocked to hear her say this, but I shouldn't have been surprised. My sister, Pat, not quite a year older than I and then a student at Radcliffe College, had participated in the 1965 protest march with Rev. Martin Luther King Jr. in Selma, Alabama. She didn't tell my parents that she was going on that march.

But before she left, she gave me a letter and included her will in case she was killed there. Thankfully, she returned.

On our way to Texas, the three of us stopped at a nice restaurant in South Carolina for lunch. After waiting and watching many others be seated before us, I complained to the supervisor. She said our turn was coming, but it never did. Finally, Astrid said, "You don't get it. They are not going to serve us because I'm Mexican." We left.

~

We first met Elizabeth (Liddy) Finn in basic training in San Antonio. She was a captain in the Army Nurse Corps and was helpful and friendly to all the young nurses. Very protective of us, she helped us understand that some of the older male officers tried to take sexual advantage of the younger nurses, so she warned us we had to be careful. In our free time, Joan, I, and some other nurses explored the sights in the area or went out to local restaurants or the officers club for dinner and dancing. We had some great times and were not aware, at first, of any officers trying to exploit us.

After basic training, we were sworn in as second

lieutenants. Many of our nursing school peers chose to go to San Francisco for their first assignment. Maybe The Mamas & The Papas' "California Dreamin'" lured them. I liked skiing and convinced Joan that we should go to Colorado with its beautiful mountains. We could always visit our friends in California, including Astrid, who asked to be stationed there. Joan agreed with my idea, and we were sent to Fitzsimons Army Medical Center in Denver, Colorado.

I asked for and was assigned to the pediatric ward. At times I was floated to other units, including the pediatric intensive care unit. Joan landed in the OB/GYN unit and was happy there. We shared a nice two-bedroom Bachelor Officers Quarters (BOQ) apartment on the quadrangle. Lots of single young people lived there. We had a great time skiing and partying.

That is where we saw Liddy again, now stationed

at Fitzsimons as an Army Nurse Corps captain and living in her own apartment on our quad. About ten years older than us, Liddy continued to be protective of all the younger nurses who were exposed to older male personnel. We probably wanted her attention and secretly appreciated it.

As we got to know Liddy better, she told us about her life. As a young teenager, she had been sent to a convent after her mother died. She planned to become a nurse and a nun. But she was mistreated and sexually abused by some of the priests there. When she was old enough, she left the convent.

The staff at Fitzsimons were cordial to the new, young officers. Once, a nice older officer, Colonel Smith, was making the rounds at the hospital and stopped to ask how I liked my assignment and what I thought could be done to improve the adjustment of new nurses to their units and to the military. He said he would like to talk more with me to discuss ways older military personnel could help younger staff, and he asked me out to dinner. I was pleased he was interested in my ideas, and I agreed to meet him later that week. He picked me up at the BOQ, and we drove to a nearby restaurant.

We were sipping wine and chatting when he received a phone call. He seemed surprised but excused himself and went to answer it. When he returned, he appeared angry and said that the caller wanted to speak with me. To my surprise, it was Liddy calling to warn me to be careful because the Colonel's intentions were not good. He had a reputation for getting young women drunk and then abusing them. She told me that she had threatened to report him if he attempted to assault me and had asked him to take me back to my BOQ immediately.

I was so naïve, thinking Colonel Smith really wanted to discuss issues of young nurses' adjustment to the hospital and to military life. By the time I returned to the table, he had paid the bill and said we had to leave. He was sullen and silent on the way back, dropped me off at the BOQ, and never spoke to me again. I learned quickly not to put myself into compromising situations. After a while, I had a sense of those men I did not want to find myself with in some isolated spot. All of us missed Liddy when she left Colorado Springs in spring 1967 to serve in Vietnam.

Liddy wrote to Joan and me often from her new assignment—as head nurse in an intensive care unit at the US Army Third Field Hospital in Saigon. She spoke about the sadness of war. Most of her patients were young GIs. Many were severely wounded and had been sent from the battlefield to receive care. When they were strong enough, they were evacuated to a military hospital in the US. Some were young teens who had stolen an older brother's identification card to join the military and serve in Nam.

During Liddy's time off, she and some of the other nurses went to Vietnamese orphanages around Saigon. She wrote that it felt good to help the children, to give them some comfort by singing to them or taking them out for an ice cream treat. I loved reading her letters.

~

In June 1967, one year after graduating from nursing school, Joan and I talked about our second assignments. She had been thinking of requesting work in California because our friends from nursing school were living there and loving it, hippies and all. I told her I wanted to volunteer for Vietnam to work with children there. She thought about it and decided she would go to Vietnam too.

When we spoke to the female military recruiter, I asked to work on a pediatric unit with Vietnamese children. She told me she doubted such a unit existed in US Army hospitals in Vietnam but agreed to mention my preference when she forwarded our requests. I was excited about volunteering for pediatrics in Vietnam because it made me feel as though I were going on a humanitarian mission.

Our parents were horrified and angry when we told them we had volunteered for Vietnam. The war was heating up in 1967, but for us it was an adventure, and we didn't dwell on fear. Our requests went through quickly and our orders were cut. Bob, one of the men I was dating then, said he would reenlist and join me. I told him not to do that but to follow his plan to attend law school. We could write to each other while I was away. Honestly, I had no plans to settle down. I was having too good a time!

Joan and I were to leave for Vietnam from San Francisco. We went a few days early to spend time with our nursing school friends who had settled there. We wandered around Haight-Ashbury and had flowers painted on our faces. Many people looked stoned. Others flashed the peace symbol. We did too with our hands in the air. We gave out flowers, carried signs that said "War Is Not Healthy for Children or Other Living Things." Some offered us weed, but we politely declined. We were having a great time participating in those anti-war activities in California. In my mind, I was not going to Vietnam to support the war but to help children.

Sandy Beaches, Pumpkin, and Ronald Colman

AS THE CHOPPER skimmed the ground, I saw the darkness below erupt into flashes of fire from predawn mortar attacks. There was no way to know who was firing at whom. Above the sound of the chopper engine, I could hear cracks and pops—gunfire directed at us. At the first glow of dawn, those sounds stopped. The soldiers were retreating from the territory, and for a few hours the area belonged to the people again.

It was early morning, and the sun was low in the sky. Joan leaned out of the chopper and began snapping pictures. In her excitement, she nearly fell out, catching herself just in time. Her camera case wasn't so lucky. We watched it float down into the China Sea. We flew over a dark green mosaic of rice paddies. The shadow of our chopper also fell over Vietnamese farmers working in the fields, dressed in black shirts and pants, walking slowly after their lumbering oxen. None of this seemed real to me. I felt as though I was watching a travelogue.

Suddenly we touched down at the 91st Evacuation Hospital. I snapped out of my reverie and looked around. The entire compound was only ten to fifteen acres. It extended a few hundred yards along a beach. Then there was barbed wire, more sand, a little village, then more sand. The only trees were a couple of scraggly palms a few feet high. Otherwise, there was no green at all. Joan stared at the sand and water with a big grin on her face.

"It's a heck of a lot better than Saigon."

I was tired and dirty and pissed at the army or myself—I was not sure which—for sending me to this hell, but I had to admit the blue water looked lovely. I had pictured teeming hospital wards, wounded GIs, bullets flying around us, but I had never imagined stepping into a brochure for a Caribbean island.

A young corpsman met us at the helicopter, took us and our duffle bags containing precious makeup and fatigues to our hooch, and dropped them off in our rooms. He said he would be outside the hooch for five minutes in case we wanted to freshen up before going to headquarters to sign in.

All GI housing and buildings were called hooches, whether they were prefabricated metal Quonset huts or wooden "jungle huts." Our hooch was wooden with a metal roof. I had been looking forward to living in a tent, which seemed very romantic to me, but instead I would be in a wood hut with a tin roof.

I took a quick look at this bare eight- by ten-foot cubicle that was to be my home for the next year. We rated our own little space because we were officers. It had a cement floor, bare walls with one nail for a hook, an army cot with mosquito netting, and a deflated rubber mattress. At least I had a room to myself.

Then I saw something that really cheered me up.

In Saigon, Liddy had to use a toilet that was a hole in the ground with a wooden plank on either side. I had imagined lots of odd things about Nam but never imagined myself standing over a hole full of feces to defecate. Here in hell and gone there were real toilets. How wonderful! They flushed! And there were also indoor individual showers. I quickly brushed my teeth with bottled water.

Several of our hooch mates introduced themselves and welcomed us. They were all close to our age. Their tans told us they had been here a while. One nurse explained that this was a junior hooch, where they put all the younger nurses. Then she opened the back door to show us how close we were to the clean white sand, the bright blue sky, and the sight and sound of the ocean waves. She explained that lifeguards were assigned during the quiet times, when swimming was allowed. Coming from Rhode Island, Joan and I both loved the ocean.

Soon it was time to go. A corpsman was waiting to take us over to headquarters. We found him lounging against the sandbags outside. He immediately flipped his cigarette away. As we walked, he told us that Agent Orange, a defoliant, was regularly spread around the fence. The chemical was known to make people sick, so it was used to keep the Viet Cong out and to prevent

Vietnamese girlfriends of some staff members from sneaking onto the compound. It was also spread around some of the nurses' barracks to eliminate a buildup of foliage.

As we approached the headquarters, I asked the corpsman what he thought of the chief nurse.

"She's okay but strict with the nurses, I hear. They call her Pumpkin."

"What does that mean?" I asked.

"You'll see," he said.

The base was quiet and the air cool.

"In you go."

He opened the door but would not come in with us. The woman at the desk didn't notice us but sat scowling at her paperwork, furiously shuffling papers and jotting down notes. Our rosy-cheeked chief nurse was just under five feet tall and about as wide. Now we understood her nickname. "Colonel Skodova" was the name on her fatigues.

She was about fifty, ancient by our standards. She stopped rustling papers to scrutinize us as we stepped in and gave the mandatory salute. Our shiny new second lieutenant bars indicated we were just out of school. Joan and I were both small and had often been mistaken for high schoolers. I could tell from the look on her face that she was wondering what we were doing here. What was she going to do in the middle of a war with these two children? When we told her our ages, she just shook her head and muttered, "The gold dust twins." We had no idea who they were, and we were not about to ask.

"Ready to meet your commander?"

Before we could answer, she stood up and took us into the next room to meet the commanding officer of the 91st. He welcomed us and passed us back to Colonel Skovoda, who would fill us in on our assignments and the regulations. Back in her office, she read the long list of regulations of proper nurse behavior. As she spoke to us, she kept removing imaginary lint from our fatigues. It drove me crazy. I kept flinching but that didn't stop her.

"Let's take a tour," she said while showing us the door. She marched us back across the compound into the hospital units, introducing us to nurses, doctors, and corpsmen. Everyone was in olive drab fatigues and combat boots. The only jewelry allowed to show were watches and chains with dog tags. She chatted about people, supplies, and the different wards, acting as though this might have been our first day in any hospital in the States.

Set up by the military to take care of war casualties, the 91st Evacuation Hospital was the first of its kind in Vietnam. Twenty units, each housed in a separate wooden hooch, holding about two hundred patients and fifty nurses. Colonel Skovoda cheerily explained that the army separated the units so that if the compound were hit, the entire hospital would not be destroyed. Sandbags lay everywhere, layered like rock walls around the sides of the hospital units. Half-buried bunkers surrounded the units and our living quarters. Because we had a helicopter unit, we were a target of the Viet Cong, who were focused on destroying the choppers.

She rushed us through the medical and surgical intensive care units, the emergency room, the operating and recovery rooms, and the graves registration unit. A cement sidewalk with a tin roof and a wooden railing connected all the units. A narrow unpaved road separated the hospital from our living quarters, which were built on the beach. Beyond our hooches lay only sand and blue ocean. About two hundred yards to the right of the officers' quarters, separated by barbed wire and mines and guarded at night by soldiers in a lookout tower, stood a small Vietnamese village. About a mile or two away on the left was the beginning of the jungle.

The 91st was an all-purpose hospital. There was a unit for wounded ARVN (soldiers of the Army of the

Republic of Vietnam) and ROK (Republic of Korea) patients. Of course, GIs were also sent to the 91st. If their wounds were minor, they would not be out of action for long.

The place was crawling with 173rd Airborne troops. They wore camouflage gear when visiting their wounded buddies. I never got used to being saluted, and these men never seemed to forget. They were young and serious, always snapping salutes and repeating their motto: "Airborne all the way, ma'am." Sometimes they shortened the motto to just "Airborne, ma'am." The spunkier ones smirked and saluted, saying, "All the way, ma'am," clearly alluding to more than their undying loyalty to the 173rd. I just smiled and half-saluted back.

As we walked from unit to unit, we became aware of the noise of choppers overhead. They were from a Dust Off unit (air ambulances called Helicopter Ambulance Medevac Units) attached to the hospital. The sound was ominous. No matter what you were doing, you would pause for a second to listen, not because of the noise but because of what it meant. Wounded were coming in. When a chopper left and returned quickly with wounded, you realized how close you were to the fighting.

We stopped in the pediatric unit full of Vietnamese

children injured by the war. What shocked me most was the size of the children and young adolescent patients. So many were so tiny and so sad-looking. Maybe this is how it would have looked if all the American children in a pediatrics unit had been in bad car accidents. Their bodies were wrapped in gigantic bandages. Often their arms and legs were in casts or splints. Their huge, serious, solemn eyes peered from their undernourished faces. I remember thinking, *These are children.* They had no place in a war zone. Standing there looking at the children, my heart melted, and all I wanted to do was stay. But Colonel Skodova was getting anxious for us to move along.

Some units had Vietnamese women to help, cleaning up after the doctors and nurses, washing instruments to go back to the OR for sterilization, straightening out cots, chatting with patients, and generally keeping them comfortable. Everyone called them *mamasans*, a GI term for a married Vietnamese woman that may have come from the Second World War but now referred to any local woman.

We stopped and rested for a bit. The Colonel had a lot of energy, but the heat bothered her, and sweat dripped from her face. "It gets to be 120 degrees in the shade, you know," she groaned. She asked us what unit we wanted to work in. I felt she was being courteous and probably already knew where she wanted us placed. But without hesitation, I said pediatrics.

"Wonderful," she said. "Most nurses think pediatrics is a punishment. They want to work in intensive care or PreOp with the GIs and the air conditioning." She sighed as she mopped her face with a large olive drab handkerchief.

She assigned Joan to the medical intensive care unit, the one with the GIs. Joan could not believe her luck. We soon learned that every nurse without a specialty rating was rotated through ICU so that the head nurse, Major Gorman, could check her out and then move her elsewhere on the compound. Major Gorman? Joan and I looked at each other. Could it be?

Major Gorman turned out to be the same person who was in our basic training class at Fort Sam Houston. She was almost six feet tall, thin, wore round metal-framed glasses, and spoke with a Boston accent. When we first met her, Joan, a veteran of the Catholic school system, whispered, "Here comes Mother Superior." First impressions may be wrong, but in eight weeks of basic training we had seen her smile twice. This was no warm reunion. "Hello" and a slight nod was all we got from Major G.

Finally, Colonel Skodova took us to the mess hall for breakfast. I felt as though I had worked an entire day. And it was only breakfast time. It was hot and bright, and everyone's eyes seemed to be on us. As we walked into the officers' dining area, a pair of eyes stood out. They belonged to a doctor seated at the table in front of ours. I was surprised when the Colonel stopped by his table to introduce us. He was an orthopedic surgeon and the second in command at the base. After I sat down, I could not stop staring at him. He was tall, tanned, handsome, and in his mid-forties with dark curly hair, a touch of silver at the temples, and a big, wide smile. He clenched a pipe in his mouth and every so often his sensuous lips allowed a little puff of smoke to escape. He was beautiful and had a deep voice. He was my Ronald Colman.

One of the younger nurses noticed my staring and whispered that Ronald Colman was involved with the head nurse on the pediatric unit. He was married, but he and the nurse had been together for a long time, ever since they met in San Francisco. I felt sorry for his wife and children. So much for Ronald Colman.

I kept getting refills from the huge coffee urn. I

was on my third or fourth cup, chatting away, when suddenly thirty-six hours without sleep hit me. I did not want to tell one more person where I had been stationed last. As I got quieter and quieter, Joan got chattier, introducing me to everyone in sight, as if she had to make up for my silence. Colonel Skodova took one look at us and told us to take the rest of the day off. We had not slept since we saw Liddy in Saigon twenty-four hours earlier.

We staggered back to the hooch. The sun was full in the sky and the temperature was climbing toward one hundred. I made it to my cubicle. My bag was unopened. I lay down on the cot with the deflated mattress, closed my eyes, and was out.

~

Joan and I woke up in the afternoon to the sound of our hooch mates laughing and chatting on their way back from work. They were friendly and introduced themselves again. We were all roughly the same age, many from New England, and some much more worldly than others.

Joan and I decided to explore more of the base and ended up in the PX. There was not much on the shelves. The supply officer, a sergeant, explained what was available there from time to time—deodorant, perfume, makeup, soda, wine, water, coffee beans, and some simple articles of clothing. Everything from chinaware to refrigerators sometimes showed up, and he promised to let us know when that happened. We found our way to the post office, where we could pick up our precious letters and packages from the US. Then we went to the officers club for a drink and dinner with some of our hooch mates. On the way back to our rooms we stopped to look at the beautiful quiet sea. I felt rested and began to feel excited about this yearlong adventure.

SUSAN HUNT BABINSKI

Pediatric Nursing

THE NEXT MORNING at 6 am, I reported for my first day on pediatrics. The hooch looked like most other wards. It was a long wooden rectangular building with a screen door at either end—a jungle hut with walls that ended three quarters of the way up with wooden posts holding up the roof. Burlap covered the open spaces to let in a little light and a breeze. The burlap-covered windows did not allow much light, but they were safer than glass and cheaper than screens. The overhanging metal roof shielded us from the heat and possible bomb fragments. The room was dark and dreary, with the only light coming from a few naked bulbs. The cement floors were continually swept, but they always seemed dirty. I could not understand why huge fans mounted on stands were silent until someone turned one on. They made a terrible racket and hardly stirred the air. Open doors in the front and back of the unit caught an occasional breeze. When that happened, it felt wonderful.

Halfway down the fifty-foot room, along one wall was the nursing station, an E-shaped counter with a medicine closet behind it. A shelf behind the station held the little equipment we had—a thermometer tray, blood pressure cuffs, and the like. The patient charts stood in a portable metal rack. On the counter was a phone that worked by picking it up, pressing a button on the receiver, cranking it, and yelling "Lifeline, lifeline" to get an operator. No one ever explained why we always screamed "Lifeline, lifeline." I suspect no one knew. It was regs.

The injured women had a unit across the ramp from peds, and when the census got low, they combined the two units. If a mother and child were both patients, we would keep them together, usually on the pediatric unit.

Compared with any hospital where I had worked before, this one was out of the stone age. There was no running water on the unit. The corpsman had to lug twenty-gallon containers to an outside faucet thirty feet away to fill them with water. The containers were heavy, but nothing compared to the portable toilet arrangement known as the honey bucket. Every unit had one, a large metal pail with a handle that was housed in a closet at one end of the hooch. Only occasionally did someone use the honey bucket. Most patients were confined to their beds and used bedpans that were dumped into the honey bucket. At the end of the shift or earlier if it were reaching the brim, a corpsman would lug it outside, dump it in a sump hole, and wash it out. When full, it weighed at least fifty pounds.

After I had been on the unit for a few days, the corpsman saw me watching him prepare to lug the bucket and noticed the look of distaste on my face. "Lieutenant, could you come here for a minute and help me carry this?" he asked. I was not going to look like a shrinking violet, so I walked over and picked it up. I did not get more than a few steps before the contents were slopping around, spilling on my uniform and boots. It weighed half as much as I did. I felt sick from the stench, the heat, and the contents. The corpsman returned and mercifully relieved me. "Thank you, ma'am," he said nonchalantly. I am not sure he needed my help, but from then on, I appreciated the corpsman lugging that bucket.

Supervisor Sue

I loved working in pediatrics from the beginning.

Captain Sue Israel, our head nurse, was wonderful. She was ten years older than I, in her early thirties, and was dating Ronald Colman. Sue was professional, somewhat distant, yet easy and pleasant to work with. What I loved most about Sue was her attitude. She did not pull rank. While she showed me around the unit, explaining procedures, she seemed more like an older sister or a friend. When I did something incorrectly, she gently showed me a better way to irrigate a wound or bandage a dressing without making me feel like an idiot. She had the same pleasant attitude to the staff, corpsmen, and *mamasans*. There always seemed to be a bunch of children tagging along behind her. While she told me about the nursing needs of the children, she kept bending down to hug or tickle one of them. It seemed she needed the physical contact and activity to hide her emotions as she told me about their wounds. I looked upon her as my role model. I hoped that in ten or fifteen years I would be as good as she was, and that my Ronald Coleman would not be married to someone else.

Corpsman Charlie

A corpsman was a cross between an aide and a practical nurse. In the field, he might even work as a doctor. He was an enlisted man and could be any rank from a corporal to a sergeant. He might be a conscientious objector, in which case he would not carry a gun. There was always at least one corpsman on the unit to help the nurses. I suspected that the army in its nineteenth-century prudery thought it unwise to leave a "helpless female" nurse alone on a ward without a big strong soldier to protect her. This arrangement meant we had fledgling nurses often in charge of corpsmen with years of experience treating wounds and tropical diseases. It was the army way.

I spent so much time with corpsman Charlie and depended on him so much that I grew closer to him than to almost anyone else on the base. The nursing supervisor and the doctors might stop by the unit for a few minutes, but during the night shift it was the two of us and the children. If one had a good corpsman, life on the wards could be a pleasure. If he was bad-tempered, life was hell. I was so lucky to have Charlie.

When Sue introduced me to Charlie, she whispered, "He's great." He looked about my age and had an open smile. He was a sergeant and probably joined the army instead of being drafted. He was not very tall and a little pudgy with straight black hair and soulful, dark brown eyes. He was from Texas and spoke with a gentle southern accent.

On my first day we didn't say very much, but I could see he loved the children, and they loved him. They were teasing him about the sweat dripping off him despite the bandana around his head. Perspiration glistened on his hair and rolled down his cheeks and neck. He made mock angry growling sounds and shook his head and sprinkled the children with his sweat while they shrieked with laughter. He was a big, sweet, gentle, caring guy.

Mamasans

I was getting used to seeing Vietnamese women scurrying around, doing all the clean-up work on the base. Some kept the officers' quarters clean and did the laundry, others helped on the wards. Many seemed indifferent to us or even suspicious, but some of the younger ones who worked in our hooch would laugh, tease us, and be friendly. That we didn't speak their language did not make our relations with them easier.

I made friends with Cho, the *mamasan* on peds. She always wore a white muslin shirt and black pants. When she came to work, she wore a full-brimmed straw hat that she carefully hung in the utility closet until the end of her shift. She was about thirty, and I don't think she was married. Cho was taller than most of the Vietnamese and very thin. She wore her brownish-black hair in a pageboy with bangs. Her light skin was sprinkled with freckles across her nose and cheeks, and she had the most wonderful smile that crinkled her face. She must have been Eurasian.

Cho's main job was sweeping up, emptying bedpans, making beds, and informally acting as an interpreter. She had good training as a nurse from a Vietnamese hospital and would occasionally help change dressings. I think she would have done more nursing care had we allowed her.

We had one metal cart for all the sterile supplies, tapes, forceps, and other small instruments. If we were not careful, it would get covered in dust. That cart was Cho's pride and joy. She kept the instruments sterile and perfectly organized. It gave me such satisfaction to see that cart so neat and complete.

Cho taught me some Vietnamese phrases and a little about her culture. I was never to beckon with my hands while saying "*Lại đây mau*," translated literally as "Come here always." One only beckoned to animals and small children. If you wanted to call politely, you held your hand upside down while waving it.

She talked to the children when we could not understand what they wanted. Through a mixture of mime, simple English, and Vietnamese, she explained to us why a child was crying. If someone was in pain, we could help. It was more difficult when a child cried for Mama. We might hug them, or Cho might sing them a song. It was all we could do.

No entertainment existed for the kids. No toys, music, radio, visits. Nothing. That is until corpsman Charlie and I started singing to them as we cleaned them and changed dressings. Those who could followed us, and some joined us phonetically in singing songs like The Mamas & The Papas' "Monday, Monday" and The Beatles' "When I'm Sixty-Four." The kids loved it. Singing and being together provided a great, happy diversion for all of us. The kids tried to teach me some Vietnamese songs and laughed at my feeble attempts. I did learn a few helpful Vietnamese phrases while trying to learn these songs. We shared magazines sent to us from the States with the children. The preteens, especially, bonded over the magazine photos of movie stars and American fashions.

The Children

On my fourth day, some of the little children who were not bedridden jumped out of bed to greet me when I came in the door. They rushed over, laughing shyly when I hugged them and spoke to them in a language they could not understand. I belonged, and that felt great. I tried to show them my pleasure through gestures and the little Vietnamese I knew. I found it easier to communicate with the children than with the adults. With the children, I interacted mainly through gesture, tones, and looks, and we became attuned to one another.

The children did not smile often. Their beautiful eyes were so sad. They rarely complained. They sat quietly on their cots and watched the activity on the unit or spoke quietly to one another. Those who were part Vietnamese and part French were the most beautiful of all. They seemed so old, but when they played, they were suddenly happy. No matter how sick or hurt they were, when playing, they forgot all that for a moment. I would do anything to make those smiles appear, however fleeting they might be.

No matter how early I came to the unit, Charlie

would already be there emptying urine foley bags and setting up intravenous (IV) injections. He would stop what he was doing and call out in his warm Texas drawl, "Good morning, Lieutenant." And I'd reply, "Hello, Sergeant." It was the ritual signal that our day had begun. A couple of the teenage girls who had learned to say "hello" in English greeted me from their beds, waving and shouting "hello" and giggling when I waved and shouted "hello" back.

In Colorado, I had seen children with asthma, croup, and leukemia, but I had never seen children torn up by bullets, grenades, or mine fragments, or burned by napalm. Often the burns covered large portions of their bodies and were infected. I learned that before transport to the hospital, the burns were covered with dung to ease the pain. However, the dung caused terrible infections.

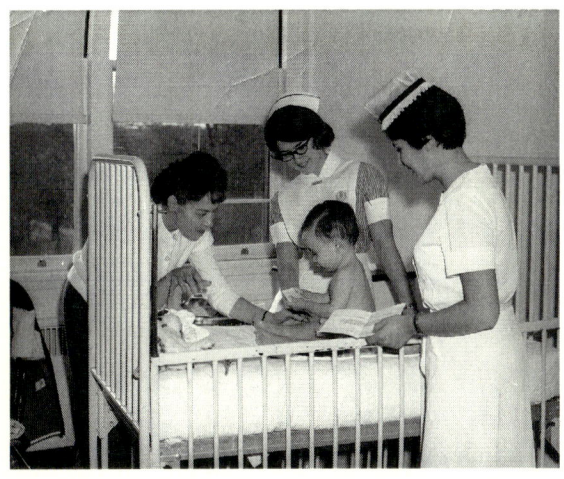

There were many medical problems. All Vietnamese had dysentery and ascaris. No one was hospitalized for that because it was as common as a cold. Worms infected the children's bodies. I pulled what looked like a six-inch earthworm from the mouth of a child who was choking on it. Worms came from every human orifice and had been known to force their way through the skin and eyeballs. I never got used to them.

A few of the children were there for elective surgery. Doctors would see them during rounds in local hospitals and bring them in for special treatment. It was good for the children and for the doctors, who had opportunities to try all sorts of operations and perfect their craft. The doctors, like the nurses, wanted to do something humanitarian aside from patching up the often irreparable wounds of war. Officially, these operations never happened because they were not war connected. But they made us feel that we were doing more than just mopping up a mess.

An older teenage girl was brought in with a large, badly infected leg, the result of an untreated frag wound. The wound stank, and I was sure I could see past the tendons and muscles to the bones. Maggots, looking like cooked macaroni, had infested her wound. In the past, maggots were commonly used to clean infected wounds of dead rotten flesh, and we were doing the same thing. We left the maggots in place, gave her clean moist bandages and systematic doses of antibiotics. Every day, the doctor and I changed the wet dressing. The maggots did their job, but the sight of them sickened me. The girl looked away whenever we changed the bandage. She was probably sickened too.

Lily

That was not her name, but it is what I called her. She was eleven years old and burned by napalm. She looked as though she had been through an acid bath. Her pock-marked skin was wrinkled and ugly, as though someone had pressed gravel into her face, removed the grit, and left a thousand tiny indentations. Her lips and eyelids were so badly scarred that she couldn't close one eye completely. We could do nothing about those problems. She was in the hospital because scarring had constricted her arms. We were trying to release them to give her greater range of motion.

When I worked on the charts at the desk, Lily would come to see me and put her arms around me. I gave her a little hug and she stood there. She was so needy. Like most of the children, she had no visitors. She seemed content to stand close to me and touch my hair. After a while, I forgot how pock-marked and disfigured she was and thought of her as another one among all the cute children in our care.

Chubby Bunny

She was bigger than most Vietnamese, always giggling and showing off her wonderful dimples. A real teenager. She didn't speak much English, and I knew very little Vietnamese, so we didn't really talk to one another. Instead, we fooled around repeating words back and forth. In a haphazard way, we taught each other a little of the languages we spoke. I teasingly called her "Chubby Bunny" one time, and she laughed, probably at the sound of the words. She wanted to know what a chubby bunny was. I tried to explain by comparing chubbiness to my skinniness, by pantomiming long ears like a rabbit jumping around. We both started laughing. She loved the sound of the words "Chubby Bunny" and my antics. The name stuck. She thought my name was funny and, laughing, she would repeat in a sing-song way, "Sue see, Sue see."

She had been admitted for shrapnel wounds and stayed with us for quite a while before her wounds healed. Joan and I taught her some popular American songs. Like all teenagers, she loved music, and sang along to "(I Can't Get No) Satisfaction" with a heavy Vietnamese accent. She had no idea what the song meant, but she caught onto pronunciation. We went over the words with her and showed her where to emphasize certain phrases. She would screw up her face and belt out lines like "When I'm sixty-four," and we would all laugh.

Her attempts to teach us Vietnamese songs were less successful. At least she kept telling us so, laughing and shaking her head "no" at our efforts.

Kim

Kim was one of the most beautiful people I had ever

seen. She had a breathtaking smile and white, white teeth. Anyone who came on the unit would notice her head-turning looks and regal charm. She was perhaps twelve or thirteen, but I did not think of her as that young.

An orthopedic surgeon had found her in one of the provincial villages. She was deformed from polio at a young age, and had become a familiar sight in her village, crawling around on her stomach, dragging herself along on two sticks.

She had surgery to help relieve muscle constriction to allow her to walk again. On top of the cast that covered her hips and legs, she wore a blue nightshirt that looked like a dress on her. She had long, shiny black hair down over her shoulders. Every morning, she would brush her hair and sing beautiful Vietnamese songs softly to herself. I would smile and come over to listen. She would stop singing and giggle, but after a moment she would start brushing and singing again.

John/Nguyen

John was not his name. If children were on the unit for a while, Charlie and I gave them American nicknames. I knew their real names too, but with American names, the children seemed more familiar to me, more like my three younger brothers back in Rhode Island. By giving the children these new names, Charlie and I felt we were adopting them into our unit family. The children thought the names were funny and laughed. It didn't occur to me at the time that I was perhaps being disrespectful of them and their culture. I wish I had taken the time to get comfortable with their Vietnamese names instead of trying to Americanize them. It is easier to try to ignore the differences among people than to understand and enjoy them.

John, or Nguyen, was about fourteen and had gunshot wounds to his shoulder. His hands had old, nasty-looking burn scars. He never smiled and seemed sad, though not hostile. He looked at you with wide-open eyes, and you tried to look inside to see what they were seeing or what they had seen. He looked at you, and you felt like crying. But we didn't speak the same language, and if we had, what would we have said to each other? What had been his losses?

Charlie and I tried to cheer him up. We cracked jokes. We marched around acting like clowns. We laughed, giggled. The other children also tried to make him laugh. They would strut around saluting like GIs. They would pretend to be soldiers carrying guns and would defend the unit from imaginary enemies bursting through the hooch door. John/Nguyen never saluted or held an imaginary gun. He would watch but never join in. It was not that he was too old for imaginary games. Somehow the child in him had been killed.

Tim/Tram

Eleven-year-old Tram—we called him Timmy—had been hit in the abdomen by fragments from an exploding mine. A piece of his bowel had been so badly shattered that it had to be removed so that the remainder of his intestine could be sutured back together.

He loved playing soldier and always took command. The little general was a skinny little boy with a GI crew cut. He was full of fun, always grinning and saluting and saying "GI Number One." The boys who could get out of bed strutted behind Tim/Tram like GIs—marching, saluting, and firing at the imaginary enemy. Tim/Tram always called Nguyen to join, and he tried, but all he could manage was to stand close and watch. Tim/Tram healed quickly and left. The unit seemed quiet without his shenanigans. Nguyen stopped hanging out with the other children after Tim/Tram left because the others didn't make a point to call him over as Tim/Tram did.

Jimmy/Jo

Jimmy/Jo was happy to be called anything as long as it meant a good meal and a warm bed without fear of something bad happening to him. He was at the hospital to have plastic surgery on his lip—the worst harelip I had ever seen. His big, expressive brown eyes always seemed to be twinkling. Even though he had no upper lip, Jimmy/Jo was very funny, continuously chattering away. When you saw all those exposed upper teeth, you just thought he had a big open sloppy smile. The doctor had found Jimmy/Jo while making check-up rounds in a local village. The villagers thought that Jimmy/Jo was blessed because of his lip.

Pham

The Viet Cong had gone into four-year-old Pham's

village, where his father was chief. They were angry because the villagers had been friendly to the American soldiers, so they killed Pham's family and then blew away his little genitals with a shotgun. He now had an empty scrotum and a shiny smooth surface in his groin. The plastic surgeon fashioned a penis out of his skin so that Pham could urinate through his tube, which was a facsimile of his actual penis. Pham always had a sad, sweet smile for everyone. No one ever came to visit him—there was no one left. Pham wouldn't know for years how much the war had taken from him.

We had no toys or playthings on the pediatric unit. One child whose village had been destroyed drew pictures of trees and huts, perhaps to remind himself of the village he had lost. I looked at his drawings and told him they were number one, just as I might praise my little brothers' drawings at home. He didn't seem to get much pleasure from his drawings or from my praise. He just kept drawing the same scene over and over as if he were trying to make the world whole again.

Born Free

If the war was quiet enough, we would have movies outdoors in the evening. In a big grassy area that separated the front and back ramp, about thirty chairs were set up. When it got dark enough, the projectionist ran the film. The only people who attended were GIs from the back units and some corpsmen. The usual fare was musicals, Disney films, and G-rated movies—nothing controversial.

Kim and Chubby Bunny loved the movies. However, a corpsman had either raped or bought sexual favors from a young female Vietnamese patient, so teenage girls could not attend alone if adult patients or corpsmen were also attending. When Kim and Chubby Bunny saw folding chairs being carried outside, they knew there was going to be a movie. Chubby Bunny would beg me all day, "Please, Susie, movie please. Susie, movie." Kim would ask shyly at first and then would bravely chime in and giggle. None of the other nurses wanted to go. Joan and I liked going with the children, so we usually ended up putting Kim on a stretcher and taking her and Chubby Bunny. It was like going to a drive-in except that we walked.

My favorite was *Born Free*. Kim and Chubby Bunny liked it too because they could understand the story. It didn't need words. When the lion went free, we all laughed and clapped. We got emotional about the baby lion. It was easier to cry for a baby lion than to cry for the wounded babies I cared for every day.

Aid and Comfort

A visiting *mamasan* from a nearby village was wet nursing a tiny six-month-old baby with a big leg cast. The child's mother had been killed by mortar fire. A five-year-old in for minor frag wounds ran over to her. He was a lively little boy, running around the unit, following us, cocking his head, and making funny faces. He stopped and stared at the nursing *mamasan*. Cho nudged me and made sucking sounds while nodding her head toward the little boy. He was begging the *mamasan* for a drink from her breast. She laughed and motioned him away. He kept laughing and asking for some milk. The other children laughed, too.

He continued to argue with her. She raised her voice, and so did he as he demanded milk. The *mamasan* suddenly told him, "Okay" and laughingly motioned for him to come over as she handed the baby to Cho. I had heard that it is common for older children to be nursed in Vietnam. He hesitated at this dare, and then, with the other children laughing and urging him on, he went over and lay in her lap and began suckling her breast. We all laughed. But then he grew quiet. His little joke became a comfort to him. He grew peaceful and nursed in earnest as the *mamasan* cradled and rocked him in her arms. Cho and I smiled at each other. I gently caressed the cheek of the baby Cho held in her arms.

It suddenly occurred to me that I had come to Vietnam for more than a year's adventure. These children were the real reason I was there. It was as if I had joined the Peace Corps. I felt happier and more at peace with myself than I had since arriving in Nam.

Evacuations

Goodbyes have always been hard for me. But in Vietnam I sometimes faced mass goodbyes. One day word would come down. The brass would start walking the wards asking you, "How many of your patients can you move?" Perhaps they were expecting some big military action that would create new wounded personnel. We never knew why it was happening, but it was our job to move out every patient who could be moved. The GIs might go to Cameron Bay or Saigon. The Korean and Vietnamese soldiers would go back to their camps. The children would go back to their families or to an orphanage. Then suddenly, there would be empty wards and row after row of empty beds. That didn't last long because the new patients would come in right away by chopper, boat, truck—the wards would start to fill up. Later, when things settled down, we brought back the children we could find to keep them safe for a while.

Rotation

One day I arrived on the unit to find two nurses on duty. I was being floated to another unit for a day. I hated to leave peds, but the change would be fun. I found myself on a back ramp ward with regular medical-surgical cases. I was still too green to go to the intensive care units (ICUs) or recovery room on the front ramp. I was helping a doctor change a dressing on a wounded Vietnamese soldier, an ARVN. The soldier winced as the dressing came off. The wound was a red, angry-looking tear in his groin. The doctor looked at him sympathetically then muttered bitterly under his breath, "These guys don't want to be here anymore than we do." I looked at him but didn't say anything. His intensity surprised me.

On the pediatric unit, it had not occurred to me that I didn't want to be here or that the doctors and even the South Vietnamese soldiers didn't want to be here. I was where I wanted to be in spite of all the pain I saw around me. Sometimes I wondered how I could bear it, this whole year. How do you look into the eyes of young children who have seen such sorrow, pain, and horror, having lost legs, parents, siblings, a whole village, everyone and everything they have ever known? I learned from them, these tiny children who had suffered so much, and yet they trusted me and found happiness in the distractions I tried to find for them and, yes, for me. My heart had not only been broken; it had been shattered. I wasn't sure it would ever be whole again. But when I looked at the depth of sorrow in the children's eyes and occasionally saw glimpses of joy and hope, they reminded me not to give up.

Daily Life

AMAZINGLY, I SEEMED to be adjusting to life in the 91st Evac. Everyone was working eight-hour shifts six days a week. It was a quiet time in our area, but no one told me that. I thought this was what war was like. After the first few days, I stopped thinking about physical danger because I had the whole army and air force to protect me.

Once the head nurse and nursing supervisor had observed us long enough to decide we were competent, Joan and I found ourselves working night shifts. Joan often worked on the women's unit across from pediatrics. Night duty was considered less desirable, but we had low seniority. I actually thought nights were great. Less supervision, less work, and we had the whole glorious day to swim and play. Soon our shifts changed from eight to twelve hours a day, six days a week, which cramped our style a little but not very much.

Mornings

After night shift came breakfast and a cup of coffee, the best meal of the day despite dried milk and powdered eggs. How I craved real milk! I found myself dreaming about ice cream. To give the mess sergeant his due, I must admit that his Danish pastry and French toast served with bacon and sausage were pretty good. The hot and cold cereals, toast, roll, jam, juice, and coffee were not so bad either. The occasional fresh fruit was fantastic. The sergeant weighed about three hundred pounds, a testament to his work. He was one of the very few heavy Americans I saw in Vietnam.

I smoked more in Nam than I had before, partly because it just went with all the talking, coffee, and soda drinking. I went from one pack a day to three. At fifteen cents a pack, it cost next to nothing. They never ran out of cigarettes at the PX. Just about everyone smoked on the pediatric ward—it was part of the camaraderie. It helped to kill time.

After breakfast, I ran back to the hooch, grabbed a towel, pulled on my bathing suit, and slipped out the back door to go for a quick dip. Alone on the beach,

I saw and felt nothing but cool and quiet. Rarely was anyone else on the beach first thing in the morning. It may have been off limits before the lifeguard came on duty, but his presence would have spoiled it for me.

The ocean here didn't smell like the Atlantic as I remembered it from Rhode Island. I thought the odor was different because the water was so clean except for the occasional feces floating by from the village next door. There were no flowers or trees nearby, so there were no natural scents on the compound except the fishy odors of the *mamasans*' lunch. The beach was so quiet, even the gentle waves were silent.

I dove into the warm, calm water, swam for a bit, and then let myself float. It was so unlike frigid New England ocean water. The water caressed me, washing away the sights of the night and the cries of the poor kid with burns over half of his body. It was just me, the sky, the water, and the beach. Finally drained and at peace, I crawled onto the beach and slept with my arm over my face to keep the sun out of my eyes.

By the time I woke from my sandy nap, I had company. Tink, an enlisted man, our lifeguard, had arrived. His deep tan, blondish-white hair, piercing blue eyes, and muscular body were a pleasure to wake up to. His entire tour was spent sitting on the beach watching us swim. Not a bad life for Vietnam. Nurses, officers, and a few enlisted men wandered down and spread out towels. My solitary party was over.

The beach was a drawing card for everyone. Even the Korean soldiers came for a swim. They were bigger than Vietnamese men and treated American women as though they were movie stars. They shared their rice wine and pickled hot cabbage with us and snapped pictures of us.

Afternoons

Back at the hooch I slept for about four hours—it was too hot during the day to sleep any longer. I slept through the *mamasans'* laughter and chatter and the doors banging while they went about their work. I usually slept through lunch. It was a quarter of a mile to the mess hall, and the food wasn't good enough for me to make the effort. Besides, they didn't allow cutoff shorts in the mess hall.

The *mamasans* were our daily maid service. They washed and ironed our uniforms, polished our combat boots, and swept and straightened our rooms. If no starch was available, they used hair spray instead. For a long time, we couldn't imagine why our fatigues were so sticky and smelled of perfume after they got damp with perspiration. Someone spotted the women ironing with hair spray and told them not to do that anymore. Hair spray was too precious to use as a substitute for starch.

The Vietnamese women who worked for us would bring their own food for lunch. They didn't eat army food. Either they didn't like it, or perhaps no one offered it to them. They went behind the nurses' hooches and started small fires on the sand. Then they put their pots on the fire to cook their fish and rice. The odor permeated our hooches. Small clusters of two or three *mamasans* tended each fire, eating and talking, squatting with their bottoms never touching the ground. They laughed and chattered in their singsong voices. Sometimes they offered us food or spoke to us. When we didn't answer because we couldn't understand them, they nodded and laughed good-naturedly.

I was reluctant to try the *mamasans'* food because dysentery was common. But sometimes, to be friendly, I took a small piece and prayed that I wouldn't become ill. They laughed at the way I nibbled at their delicacies. The food tasted okay, but the odor was terrible. I remember one unbelievably foul-smelling dish they called *nuoc mam*. I asked Charlie later what it was and was sorry to learn it was fish heads buried in the ground, where they fermented and were later dug up and served on rice.

Party Time

After lunch, whatever time that was, we dressed in civvies for partying. I tried not to wear fatigues off duty because they reminded me of work. One cute guy told me fatigues were sexy. That may have been a line, but I liked it. Maybe it was like wearing your boyfriend's pajamas. No one could convince me that those olive drab baseball caps we had to wear were anything but ugly. I didn't wear mine if I could help it, and generally jammed it into one of the large pockets on the side of my fatigue pants. Joan told me that one of these days the good old Colonel would catch me, and I would pull KP duty. I didn't care what Colonel Skodova might do. I refused to wear it, and it became a running joke on the compound.

Most of us younger nurses wanted to party as much as possible. We went off the base, even under tightened security or when told to stay on base. The area was getting dangerous, but the rewards of going off base were too tempting. Off the base, we got to meet Air Force men. They had flair—champagne taste on combat pay. They did not have a long life expectancy. Someone or something was bound to shoot them out of the sky, so they lived like there was no tomorrow.

Because these suicidal types were rare to attract into the Air Force, the military treated them very well. Their quarters were air-conditioned, wood paneled, and equipped with the latest appliances. When we visited, they served melon balls in champagne flown in from the Philippines. Nothing was denied them. Beneath their high life was the statistic that only fifty percent would make it back home.

When the airfield was built, more money was put into officers' quarters, lavish rooms, stores of whisky, and better food than the rest of the base had. The money ran out long before the field was finished, so they had to request more funds, and they always got it. The runway was the last thing to be built.

Sometimes a few of the other nurses and I went for unauthorized airplane rides with the pilots when they delivered supplies to refugee camps. We would fly along the shoreline, practically surfing the waves. Occasionally we saw brilliant flashes of light and heard the popping sounds of gunfire directed at us, but we just laughed. Despite any evidence to the contrary, not for a minute did I allow myself to think anything bad might happen to us.

Back on the base I had plenty of diversion between the beach and the officers club. I played pool with nurses and doctors in the recreation hut and began to develop great bank and combination shots.

Some nurses were not interested in partying. Jackie, who roomed across the hall from me, did not go out socially. She kept almost completely to herself, spending all her spare time in her room, writing letters to her fiancé, reading, listening to classical music, and sleeping. Joan and I stored Cokes in her refrigerator, which gave us an opportunity to get to know her. Jackie worked in the OR, trying to patch up the mangled bodies of soldiers and civilians. Although she was only a few years older than us, she seemed ancient, a tiny woman with short dark hair and big blue eyes that she hid behind thick glasses. She made no attempt to fix herself up. She never took off her floppy sloppy fatigues. In her room she dressed in rolled-up fatigue pants, a khaki tee shirt, her dog tags, and a pair of cloth thongs. She generally had a non-filtered Lucky Strike in one hand and a rum and Coke in the other. She never partied.

Dating

I dated several officers during my yearlong tour in Vietnam. Some were unlike anyone I had ever dated before. I had a sense that anything I did in Nam was strictly for fun or for forgetting. Many of us felt that way. There were few Vietnamese women in relation to the number of American men. As a result, nurses got a lot of attention. It was flattering to think you were Miss America, forgetting that you were one of only a few women within hundreds of miles. The men from the 173rd Airborne unit, the engineering units, and the battalions that passed through our area all stopped by to see us and the Vietnamese women. Out here we were all movie stars. I got tired of guys telling me that I was like their girl back home even though I knew this was their idea of a compliment.

The officers club was the place to hang out in the evening. This windowless wooden structure was built on the beach not far from the ocean. As you walked in the door, off to the right was a bar with stools. There was plenty to drink. Men from other units would come to the club for drinks and to check out the nurses. The bartender, a sergeant, played taped music, and people got misty singing. Generally, there were some tables filled with married doctors playing bridge. Sometimes a male nurse would join them, but never a woman. These were serious bridge players, and no women were allowed. Chatter and cigarette smoke filled the room. A foot-high platform served as a dance floor. Sometimes no one was dancing, while at other times the place was jumping with guy after guy cutting in to dance with you.

I first saw Roger at the club. He was tall, blond, and kept staring at me, but he didn't ask me to dance. For several days he just sat, nursed his drink, and watched me. He knew I had noticed him. From his jumpsuit uniform, I knew he was a fly boy, but he seemed much quieter than the other pilots I had met. After a while, we felt we knew each other by osmosis. He finally got over his awkwardness and asked me to dance. Little by little he talked more about himself and told me he came from a wealthy family that owned a drugstore chain. He was not trying to impress me, just letting me know who he was.

One night he invited me to a Broadway musical. I was not quite sure what he meant, but I promised to dress for a night out. Freshly showered, wearing a pretty cotton dress and sandals, I waited for him at the hooch. He met me with a bottle of cold white wine in his hand and two wine glasses hooked onto his pockets. He escorted me to a well-lit but deserted area on the compound near the main headquarters. It was too bright for making out and too isolated for anything else. What was going on?

With a flourish, he uncorked the wine and asked me to taste it. It was not bad at all. We walked back and forth, chatting and drinking. He pointed out the Broadway theater billboards we were passing. "Oh look! There's *My Fair Lady*. Oh, my God! *Bye, Bye, Birdie*. We've got to see that one." Finally, we chose a show. He sat me down and, in a beautiful tenor voice, sang as many songs as he could remember. He filled in with dialogue, acting out as many roles as he could fit in that one wild body. It was a crazy, wonderful evening out. Occasionally, someone would see us and be amused, but we ignored them, and arm in arm, sipping our wine, we continued our parade down Broadway.

Broadway shows were addictive. So was Roger. We started to see each other just to talk or have a drink. His tour of duty was almost up, and suddenly he was not there. I missed him and our nights on the town, but not for long. There were plenty of other men around, and I didn't have time or the inclination to sit around and pine.

I first met Stan when he stepped out of a helicopter. He was a good-looking, muscular chopper pilot who flew one of the generals around Vietnam. One day, he landed on a large sandy area near the hooches, not at the usual helicopter area. Several of the brass got out and went to headquarters. I stood there with several hooch mates, watching. Stan was the last one to leave the chopper. He jumped down and, staring directly into my eyes, walked over to me. It was as if I were there to meet him, and he had come to see me. He came on strong from the beginning, standing close and talking intimately about how I had made his trip worthwhile. It was a stupid conversation, but I could feel myself responding. No guy had ever come on to me like this. We were an unlikely pair, but I loved his physicalness and his obvious longing for sexual contact. Passions were stirred in me that I had never felt so strongly before.

I invited him in for a cold Coca-Cola. I could see his navigator smirking with some of the crew from the chopper as we walked into the hooch. We only had time for a short chat, two smokes, and a gulped Coke. One of his crew hollered into the hooch that it was time to go. We stood up, and he kissed me hard. As he left, he said he would be back. I could hardly wait.

We started seeing each other. I had never been out with anyone so macho. Thinking of him was enough to get me going. I loved how easily he lifted me and twirled me around as he kissed me passionately. He never wore underclothing beneath his fatigues, and he would slide me down along the heat of his body, and his large hands would caress me and massage my hips into throbbing putty. He was so strong and sensual. Every time he had to leave, I couldn't wait for his return. Just the thought of him would make me ache. Joan couldn't stand him. She thought he was a jerk and could not believe I was so involved with him.

His friend told me that Stan's wife and baby had died in a car accident several years ago, and that he had fallen in love with me because I reminded him of his deceased wife. His wife and baby could have been alive and well, but in Nam everyone else seemed to be dying and dead, so his story didn't seem so farfetched. Joan said that many of the guys out here invented stories that their friends would back up. You could make up any reality you liked in Nam. You only had to live it for a year.

I felt sorry for the married men. Some just enjoyed the freedom from the responsibilities of wives and children and found female companionship and solace with one nurse or another. Some married doctors stayed strictly to themselves, playing cards or pool with other male doctors, writing letters back home, reading, swimming, and some drinking heavily. Some hardly spoke to the nurses, as if to remain true, they must not have a real, non-professional conversation with a woman. Married and older soldiers were not well suited for life in a war zone.

Someone Special

I met Jerry at the beach. He was a couple of years older than I, a medical evacuation helicopter pilot assigned to a Dust Off unit that picked up wounded from the battlefield and transported them to the 91st Evacuation Hospital. He and Jim, one of his crew, spent more and more time with Joan and me. I loved listening to Jerry's stories about rescuing the injured. He was kind, intelligent, and always a gentleman. He was married and often spoke of his wife. I loved him as a friend but knew he was never going to be anything more. By being with me, Jerry was not teased by the other GIs, as he might have been if he hadn't had a girlfriend in Vietnam. As a good Catholic girl, I felt guilty because I coveted him so. He always behaved properly, being true to his wife back home.

In Jerry I had met a friend I could talk with. When I said I didn't know whether to cry or get angry or become hysterical about this crazy war, he understood my feelings. He said he felt many of the same things. We spent hours sipping Cokes, smoking, and talking. Joan said I was falling in love with him. I liked him a lot, but I knew he was married, and it stayed platonic.

Mail

Thank God we got mail twice a day. I looked forward to it in a way that astonished me. I read letters at least three or four times. I always carried an old letter with me whenever I checked the mail to comfort me if I didn't get anything. I noticed I was not the only one who carried an old letter when they came to the post office.

People back home were generous, and I received a

lot of mail and packages. My friend Pat sent several dozen homemade cookies in a large carton protected by popcorn. The chocolate chip cookies were still fresh and not crumbled at all. After putting some aside for Joan and my hooch mates, I brought the rest to the pediatrics unit. Charlie and the children dove in. The children had no sooner finished with the cookies than they began eating the unsalted popcorn. I gave them the box full of slightly stale popcorn to finish off. Soon, I heard a large commotion and saw the children opening tiny bottles and drinking something. I had not realized that Pat had sent more than cookies. Buried deep in the popcorn lay eight miniature bottles of Sicilian Gold liquor. Fortunately, not one of the kids got sick.

Early in my tour, I had written to my hometown paper, *The Evening Bulletin*, asking for donations of clothing and combs and toys for the children. My effort paid off. Members from the senior citizens center in Providence saw my published letter and decided to answer my request. I received lots of packages, sometimes with a little note tucked inside, blessing me or praising my patriotism in a sweet shaky handwriting. After each package arrived, I wrote a short note thanking the lady who sent it and telling her an anecdote or two about the children.

One day an Air Force man stationed in Tuy Hòa dropped off a special care package for me. He told me that his mother and mine had met at the Warwick Library in Rhode Island. When his mother learned that I was stationed in Nam, she offered to have her son bring some things for me. My own mother sent me things I had sounded wistful about in my letters —a popcorn maker and popcorn kernels, oil paints, paint brushes, and canvases. I used to enjoy painting portraits and landscapes. I made the popcorn, but I never used the paints. In Vietnam, I didn't want to be alone, and when I paint, I am alone.

A lot happened around the mailroom. One of the corpsmen got a Dear John letter from his wife. He had no idea of the contents when he opened the letter with his buddies all around him. He kept saying, "Oh, my God! No. Oh, my God! No." He couldn't accept what he was reading. He looked so angry and bitter. I never saw him smile again.

I wondered what a letter like that meant to a man in the field. Would he give up and get blown away? Would his anger and hatred make him a better soldier? If they let him go home with his gun, would he kill someone? Did he get high and stay that way? When everything else seems crazy and pointless, your feelings of trust and love for those at home make it possible to endure. Even if those feelings are somewhat illusory, what can it be like when you no longer have them?

One nurse received two packages marked plainly "One" and "Two." A letter asked her not to open the second until she heard the tape enclosed in the first. The tape was a marriage proposal and the second was a large diamond ring. Her fiancé was a young West Point graduate and career soldier. It seemed so romantic that he proposed to her in a battle zone. That he wasn't there was probably an indicator of what their marriage would be like. In their marriage, there might be more mail than male.

I was petrified when, on my birthday, the day after Valentine's Day, I received a small package from one of my stateside boyfriends. Fortunately, it was a beautiful watch and not a ring. I was enjoying lots of company in Nam and was not inclined to limit myself to one person, never mind to someone halfway around the world from me.

Adventures with Charlie

DESPITE MY ACTIVE SOCIAL LIFE, Charlie, the corpsman, was my closest friend besides Joan and Jerry. I had fun with the others, but they didn't know me the way Charlie did. He and I shared our love of children and our love of the work we did. We were kidding around on the ward one shift, and he asked me if I would like to go out for a steak dinner. "Sure. I'd love a big juicy steak about that thick." I showed a two-inch gap with my fingers. He smiled and said he would get us some steaks.

I agreed to meet him after dark on the back side of the mess hall. I began to have misgivings as I waited for him in the dark. We had to go to his end of the compound to get the steaks, and officers were not supposed to go into the enlisted area. After a few minutes, Charlie arrived and led me to the enlisted men's side. We kept ducking behind buildings so no one would see us. Then he had me wait under a hooch. An overhead light allowed me to see the outline of many pairs of legs walking around. I could hear music and sounds of male laughter and beer cans opening. Perhaps the NCOs were having a cookout. I had no idea where I was.

Charlie arrived carrying two plates of hot beans and thick steaks oozing juice. We found a dark place on the side of a bunker with just the moon and the occasional white flare to light the area as the soldiers on watch checked for Viet Cong. It was a quiet time, and the bombs sounded far away. We ate and talked and watched as the flares on tiny parachutes of pure silk lazily floated down.

He never did tell me how he managed to get those two medium-rare steaks. After eating for weeks in the mess hall, this was like a meal at the Four Seasons in New York City. Being forbidden to socialize with enlisted soldiers and flaunting basic army regulations made the steaks even juicier and more delicious. We did that only once. It was too risky, and we knew if we got caught, Colonel Skodova would not take kindly to it.

Charlie was my friend, always listening to my complaints and wishes. During the summer while we were on the unit, I told him I wished I had a space to hang my things. Nail hooks were far from a closet. "If y'all want a closet, then we'll make one," he drawled. About a week later, he showed up at my hooch with an armload of wooden boards. The glamor of roughing it in a war zone had worn off, and I was ready for some comforts.

He began stockpiling nails and pieces of plywood in my room until he had enough to build the closet. He found the necessary wood, nails, and tools to do the job. In our time off, we would come to my hooch so we could work together on our project. I held the boards and handed him the nails while he sweated, sawed, and hammered away. Charlie was good with his hands.

That closet became the center of our lives for a month. We talked about it on the unit, we planned the wood searches and the building schedule during our cigarette breaks. It took time and work to get the doors to slide back and forth smoothly. If it bothered the brass that an enlisted man and an officer were spending time together, no one said anything.

One day there it was—a five-foot-high, three-foot-long, and two-foot-deep standing closet with sliding doors. It looked like a Victorian chiffonier to me. There was wood left over, and Charlie asked if I would like a cabinet for my personal property. He designed a small square box with a hinged door and mounted it on the wall of the hooch. It had a padlock and key. I called it my medicine cabinet.

The furniture looked great, too special to leave unpainted. Charlie asked, "What color?"

Half-jokingly, I said, "Red." Nothing on the compound was painted red.

"You want red. I'll get you red."

I can't imagine where he got that oil-based paint. We painted both pieces of furniture fire engine red. The odor of the fresh paint was so strong I spent a couple of nights on a mat in Joan's room.

Despite the small size of my room, I managed to fit quite a few things into it. Mother sent a red bedspread and some red and white gingham checked cloth from which I made drawstring curtains to hide the burlap window. To the right was my wonderful red closet that took up most of the wall. To the left was a small white porcelain refrigerator stocked with chocolate candy, a jar of peanut butter, and lots of cans of soda.

A small woven basket containing colorful military scrip that looked like Monopoly money sat on top of the refrigerator. The army issued spending money in the form of military scrip to discourage black market trading, but there was not much to buy at the PX, and the money was useless anywhere else. In the absence of flowers, the scrip added a little color to my room.

My cot stood against the wall on the other side of the refrigerator. My cousin Kathy sent me a picture of my parents, my two blonde-haired brothers, and herself at the family's rented summer cottage at Green Hill Beach, Rhode Island. I carefully tacked it up on the wall with a colorful photo calendar of American scenes. A small yellow bamboo mat smelling like hay lay on the cement floor in front of my bed. On the wall beside the calendar hung the locked red medicine chest where I kept all my treasures, most important of which were my letters from home. We had been told not to leave letters lying around. Viet Cong, who could be your hooch maid, were supposedly known to take names and addresses off the envelopes and send official-looking letters to the States saying that the person had been killed or was missing in action.

I bought a small, silly-looking goose-necked reading lamp from the PX and placed it on top of my refrigerator. I read a fair amount that year. My reading was eclectic—Capote's *In Cold Blood*, Hemingway's *A Moveable Feast*, and Thurber's *Carnival*, to name a few. I eventually bought a small fan that circulated the air in my room a bit. What was worth the most to me was a real bed. It had a metal frame and a thin mattress. I had forgotten by then how hard and uncomfortable the cots were. Long ago, I had given up trying to keep the air mattress blown up. My new bed was a sheer joy. I now slept better than I had since coming to Nam. All these luxuries came after Charlie outfitted my little room.

Sunrise and Censure

THE ATTACKS USUALLY wouldn't start until late, after midnight. There would be gunshots, the rhythmic thumping of mortar fire, and the whistling of heavy artillery. Either our base was under attack, or the air strip or some groups of men were getting fired upon. The sounds went on and on. Sometimes we saw red flares shoot up—a red alert—meaning the enemy had infiltrated our perimeter. Somewhere, close by, enemy soldiers were coming. The shelling intensified, and we waited for it to stop.

By the end of summer, the red alerts came more frequently and seemed to go on longer. We now had to wear heavy flak jacket vests and metal pot helmets. But I still didn't feel that I was in danger. I was surrounded by an army. What could happen to me? My personal sense of safety was only shaken when an Air Force officer handed me a handgun and urged me to keep it in my room in case Viet Cong came in the door.

Whenever there was a red alert, all the hospital units with burlap windows would be in mandatory blackout. You had to stumble around in the dark with only a dim flashlight, gathering the children and putting them on the floor under their beds. For a while, the red alerts happened every night. They became so common that we would routinely go around at bedtime, putting the children on the floor, arranging pillows and blankets to make the hard, ungiving cement as comfortable as it could be.

Then we just watched the children, sat with them if they woke up, changed bandages, gave out meds, checked dressings, took temps and blood pressures, and smoked endless cigarettes while, through the burlap windows, we watched the red flares shoot into the sky near us and gently sail down, lighting up the ground. We sat and talked and smoked and waited—there was nothing else to do. At last we would hear a great whoosh, the noise of the white flares being shot off to tell us all was well. At other times nothing happened until the first glow of dawn appeared. Then the thumping of the guns stopped, and we got busy with our routines on the unit.

Charlie and I were a team. He never seemed uncomfortable about my being an officer or angry about my privileged position. We became quicker and quicker at changing dressings together. Carried away by the night and our efficiency, we began to play out little scenarios. He was a doctor. I was a doctor.

"Well, Dr. Kildare, what do you make of this?"

"What idiot did this suturing? I'll have him run out of the profession."

We made faces and pantomimed so the children could join in the fun. I watched Charlie change a dressing on a girl's leg that had been badly burned. It was a beautiful job. He not only made a neat dressing, but he treated the girl gently and carefully.

"Beautiful, *Herr Doktor!*" giving my impression of a Viennese physician.

"*Danke schön.*"

Charlie winked and managed to click his heels while still bent over, wrapping the dressing. The girl was eleven or twelve and began to giggle. He smiled and immediately clicked his heels again.

"But of course, *Doktor*. What else would you expect?"

Sometimes we even managed to forget to think

about the gaping infected wounds we were so carefully tending.

Around dawn, when we were cleaning up, changing the children's bedding, getting ready for the change from the night to the day shift, Charlie would take out the honey bucket, dump it, and rinse it outside at a pipe with running water. With the door open, the morning light flooded into the hooch.

One morning Charlie called me out back to see something. There it was—the sunrise. I had never seen such a sunrise before. So many colors. So brilliant. We leaned on the railing of the ramp outside the open back door and watched the sun rise while sharing a cigarette. The children who could walk came over and stood with us, watching the sunrise silently with us. It was quiet and cool outside, with a mild morning breeze caressing our faces. This was the coolest part of the day. The only heat we felt was from the closeness of our bodies.

From that day on, when I worked nights with Charlie, we always watched the sun come up. It became a ritual, and we worked out a system. We would try to get everything done, everyone washed and cleaned up a little earlier. The children and the *mamasans* understood and pitched in to help finish on time so that we could all have our five minutes of bliss together.

Charlie and I and whichever patients were able, and probably some who should not have gone outside because they were on bed rest, would go out the back door of the hooch. We put Kim, the lower half of her body still covered with a large cast, onto a gurney and wheeled her out so she could watch the sunrise with us. Sometimes she hummed softly while we watched, other days she just watched in silence with the rest of us.

We all sat close together on the ramp, hunkered down the Vietnamese way, or we sat on the wooden guard rails as we watched the sun rise. Charlie and I shared cigarettes with the *mamasan* patients. We could not communicate in many ways, but the shared cigarettes and watching the sunrise together were communication. To an outsider, we would have looked like a motley crew. But for at least those few minutes, we were one beautiful family. No matter what happened at night, no matter what terrors we felt yesterday, everything was washed clean for a minute while we shared the sweet morning wind, the sunrise, and a cigarette.

The sun was up and so were the children. Time to recheck dressings for drainage and add finishing touches to grooming—a braid in a little girl's hair, new used clothing from the States. I loved to dress the children in my brothers' outworn shirts and pants, which my family sent me. It was strange to see the children in my little brothers' clothing. It made me love the Vietnamese children even more. It made them more familiar. The children liked it too, or maybe they liked it because I liked it. I missed my little brothers. Most of all when I saw those cute big-eyed children strutting around in my brothers' plaid shirts.

~

One day I got a bombshell right after going off duty. Sue, my head nurse, and I walked back toward the nurses' hooches together. We were making small talk about the day's events when she said, "Hey, why don't you come over to my hooch for a cigarette and soda?" We sat on her cot and drank a couple of sodas and laughed, and then she told me she had received word from the chief nurse that Charlie and I had to "cease and desist from seeing one another."

   I couldn't believe what she was saying and started to cry. I was so tired and angry. I told her what I did in my free time was none of the army's business and that I would see him regardless of what anyone said. She just smoked her cigarette, looked at me dispassionately, and let me blow up. I could tell she didn't like this restriction any more than I did, but it was what the brass wanted. They didn't bother you about a lot of things. You could get drunk and go out with a married officer, but army rules had to be obeyed. The brass would get to you about the length of your hair, wearing the proper uniform and the required hat, and fraternizing with enlisted personnel. Perhaps they felt out of control about everything else around them and needed to exert control somewhere. They acted as though they were line officers who needed to enforce discipline with their troops. But we were hospital personnel, and no matter what the army wanted us to believe, we were nurses.

I was not angry at Sue. She liked Charlie, and she talked to me like an older sister would talk to her younger sister. She warned me that if Charlie and I continued to meet, the army would make sure we were separated by transferring one of us to another billet, possibly one worse than this one. I said I didn't care if I had to go deeper into a battle zone. She touched my arm and said gently, "You don't get it, Susan. You are the officer. If they punish anyone, it is not going to be you. Charlie is the one who will get a lot worse transfer." If we didn't stop seeing each other, he would be sent to a field combat zone.

I decided not to tell Charlie about my talk with Sue. I'm not sure why. He liked Sue, and I didn't want him to stop liking her or to act out in some way. I also didn't want to hurt him or for him to stop being my friend. It was just easier to cool our relationship without saying anything. But how would I act around Charlie when we were working together on the unit?

I didn't have to decide right away. An unwashed piece of lettuce saw to that.

Enemies

I COULDN'T BELIEVE it was possible for a person to get so ill so quickly. We had been warned about dysentery and malaria, and I had tried to use precautions. I always took the large orange pill served on Mondays in the mess hall to prevent malaria. We were warned that if we didn't take the prophylactic pill, we could be charged with an Article 15—discretionary discipline by a commanding officer. Chloroquine gave some people such serious nausea, diarrhea, and cramps that not taking the prevention seemed worth the risk of the disease itself or of the official reprimand. I took half a pill because I was small. I weighed about 110 pounds when I joined the army, but since being in Nam, I was down to 103 pounds.

    I didn't get malaria, but I woke up one day with the

most terrible cramps. I crawled over to the hospital, where they took one look at me shivering and running to the john and they knew what I had. When they took a stool sample, they found amoebic dysentery and ascaris (giant round worms).

I thought about the food samples I took from the *mamasans*, but I didn't think this was the cause because there were cases breaking out all over the camp among people who had never come near local food. I didn't get it from the tiny bits of Vietnamese food the *mamasans* gave me but from the mess hall, where they served locally grown lettuce. They had not washed the lettuce carefully enough. Half the unit was in bed.

I was asked if I needed to be in the hospital, but I said no. The privacy of my room seemed better than a hospital unit. I hardly remember anything from those first days of being ill. I rolled up into a small smelly ball on my bed, rocking back and forth and praying the cramps would stop. I finally fell asleep holding myself, only to be awakened by one of the younger, more friendly *mamasans* spraying my room with hair spray while singing a Vietnamese song. I screamed at her to leave me alone and then cried and rocked myself to sleep. I was so miserable.

The doctors treated me with piperazine and

tetracycline, neither of which helped my GI tract. After a few days, the cramps grew less frequent, and I was getting better. My first venture outside after a couple of days in bed was met with horrible pain. The medication made me photosensitive. The sunlight rendered me blind for a moment. In excruciating pain, I felt tears running from my eyes. Thank goodness Joan was with me and helped me through this illness and its effects.

I soon felt well enough to return to work despite the cramps. When I had to go to the john, I couldn't run fast enough. There was not enough time to get to the OR flushing toilet between the first cramp and the inevitable intestinal explosion. There was barely time to get to the honey bucket on my unit. For days, I made sure I was never more than twenty feet from that bucket. This illness made me feel vulnerable to the grenades, bullets, and rockets, which hadn't phased me before I got sick.

The Face of the Enemy

Without Charlie as a kind of buffer, the gap between work and play grew more distinct. At work all I thought of was work, and at play all I did was play. But the children were always with me.

The army opened a prisoner of war unit to house

the increasing number of Viet Cong and North Vietnamese Army casualties. It was surrounded with barbed wire, and the officers stationed guards inside the hooch and at the front gate. Then the army began bringing us Viet Cong children, placing them in pediatrics instead of in the prisoner of war unit. Some of the nurses and corpsmen were furious because they felt these children were enemies and belonged in the POW unit. I was warned by the corpsmen and the nursing supervisor not to become too friendly with the enemy. I heard stories of children coming up to GIs and pulling the pin on a grenade or of the Viet Cong wiring the children as walking mines. A child would beg for candy, and the GI would give them a chocolate bar, and the child would pull a cord and blow up both of them. Soldiers who saw sweet-faced children and young women throw bombs at the troops never trusted any of them again.

The fear was catching. Friend and foe looked alike. I found myself being cautious around the Viet Cong children, watching them carefully, looking for hidden strings and bootstraps. One day I was watching the Viet Cong children, and they and the other children were marching around in the clothes sent by the senior citizens from Rhode Island. They were playing soldiers and shooting at an imaginary enemy. It struck me that a five-year-old is a five-year-old. He doesn't have any politics. Without adults to wire his body, he is no more dangerous than any other child.

We

We knew so little about what life was like for the children outside the hospital. We knew about their wounds but not how they got them or who was with them when it happened. What did they think about, worry about? What was their family like? Who were their brothers and sisters? What was their village like? Was anyone at home still alive?

Sometimes the children's parents and relatives stopped by during visiting hours. They usually came from quite some distance, so they didn't visit often, but there were more visitors in pediatrics than in all the rest of the hospital. GIs were always stopping by for a moment to say hello. They loved the children, who were cute and had nothing to do with war. Dignitaries would come by as well. Because this was the army's first civilian war casualty hospital, it was a show place, and important visitors came from all over to be marched through our compound and, of course, our little pediatrics unit. I wondered whether the PR was what the army expected. Seeing all those little bodies broken by bullets and bombs must have been a reminder to everyone that the war was about more than enemy soldiers.

I got to know Kim during the months she stayed with us waiting for her huge cast to be removed. Her parents visited several times. They were leaders in their village. Her father worked closely with an American Special Forces advisor. Kim's family lived a distance from the hospital, so when they came, the advisor accompanied them. They were flown in by an American Special Forces unit.

Kim's parents were in their late twenties or early thirties. They brought her little presents like combs, picture books, and delicacies to eat. There were no chairs for visitors, so they sat on her bed. Her mother combed her hair, and they chatted and laughed. I envied the advisor's fluent Vietnamese and the warm camaraderie he had with Kim and her parents. He was a good-looking, intelligent gentleman who always let me in on what they were saying, which made me feel a part of this little family.

One day, after Kim had been with us on the unit for some time, the advisor came to see her, bringing some fruit and candy, and a cute, decorated mirror. Kim's parents were not with him, but he often came alone when he was in the area. This morning he looked a little strained. After his usual hellos, he asked if we could step out of the ward a moment. I couldn't imagine what was wrong, but I felt a terrible dread rising in the pit of my stomach.

"Her village is gone," he told me without a trace of emotion. "The whole village was destroyed."

It was so strange the way he phrased it, as if the village had destroyed itself.

"Her family?" I asked.

He didn't say anything. I knew then that Kim was an orphan.

I could feel the anger rising in me as I asked whether it was the Viet Cong or the North Vietnamese Army who had done it. He hesitated and then said, "In a way the VC." I didn't understand what he meant. I was so shaken I pressed him to tell me more so I could understand. He looked at me for a long moment and told me his company had totaled the village because it was so infested with Viet Cong. There was nothing else they could do.

He saw the look in my eyes and stared at me. "It couldn't be helped," he said. "We had to do it. It's war."

When he said "we," I suddenly felt short of breath. He didn't say "the army had to do it." He said "we." That included him and me.

We walked back in silence. From the far end of the ward, I watched, barely able to read the temperatures on the thermometers I was taking out of the children's mouths. I was just going through the motions of my work and noticing nothing but the two of them.

I waited to hear her scream and cry. I planned to go over and just hold her while she cried, while we both cried. But nothing happened. The advisor visited with Kim, and they laughed and joked in Vietnamese. He gave her the little gift of fruit and chocolate. He was loving and tender with her. He couldn't have been sweeter.

My mind was racing. A minute ago, I believed that no civilized human being would destroy a whole village. Only the enemy did that, not this nice man. Only the VC or the NVA. Suddenly it was us. We killed her parents. We were the enemy. The room spun around. I couldn't be sure of anything. Working with the children had made me very protective of them. But how could I protect them, knowing this? How could I protect Kim?

As he was leaving, I felt compelled to ask him whether he had told Kim what had happened. He didn't look into my red, tear-filled eyes as he shook his head no. I didn't tell her either. I was so angry and ashamed.

After the news about Kim's village, I felt even closer to her. But every time she would laugh or tease me, I remembered my guilty secret. Kim didn't stay in the unit much longer. She must have wondered why her parents hadn't visited or why the advisor never came back. As far as I know, Kim left the hospital thinking she was going home to her parents, her relatives, her friends, her village. What would her life be like now? Who was going to love her now?

It suddenly occurred to me that these children didn't know what life had been before the war. What must it be like to grow up with war as a normal part of your life? All they had ever known was bombs, fire, soldiers, orphanages, and death. There was no good side. Both sides were blood stained. There was no way we could have been right after we decided to destroy a village because we thought some of the inhabitants were dangerous. Whether I liked it or not, if I were to die in Vietnam, a metal emblem of a rifle would be placed on my coffin.

I was not just a healer. This was not the Peace Corps or a humanitarian mission. I was part of the United States Army. Some of us worked in the fields, some in the jungle, some in airplanes, and some in hospitals. We were all part of the war machine. Me too. I was a part of "we."

SUSAN HUNT BABINSKI

Doing and Dying

THE MONSOON SEASON began. It rained all the time. Everything around me seemed to be shifting and changing too fast. Joan got tense with cabin fever, the season, and the fatigue as our workloads continued to increase. In an act of frustration or defiance, she cut the restraint cuffs off a GI when she could not find the key.

I had one last talk with Charlie in the bunker where no one could see us. I was nervous about being seen with him and frightened of the rats that lived in the bunker. I had to get out of there, and I never told him why I had cooled off our friendship so suddenly.

My nursing supervisor and her boyfriend arranged a blind date for me with an Air Force pilot named George. The four of us broke regulations and went on a trip to Tuy Hòa City, about ten miles from our compound. This was my first time away from wounded bodies in a couple of months. It was a different world out there.

George and I started seeing each other regularly. He always carried a slingshot with him. I had no idea why. One night he began shooting out the lights along the mined area near the officers club. The men on guard duty went wild and began shooting up red flares. I asked him why he did it. He shrugged in an angry way and said it was to give the guard on duty something to think about. I think he was angry that we were generally much safer than he was in his bomber. He told me that the only people the NVA wanted to capture more than the US pilots were the female personnel. They wanted to retaliate for the barbaric treatment of captured Viet Cong and North Vietnamese Army women, whom he said were routinely raped, abused, and killed—treated far worse than captured VC or NVA soldiers. George scared me a little, but he was never dull. Whatever he did was daring and zany.

He disliked Colonel Skovoda because she gave the nurses a hard time. He wanted to paint a big pumpkin on top of the chief nurse's residence so he could buzz it and drop things on it when he flew over it. I thought he might do it, but he never did. His friend

Bill was shot down by a rocket. I knew Bill, who had a wife and children back home. His family mourned him officially but not more than his girlfriend, Sally, a nurse. This was the first time someone I knew socially was killed in Nam. The war was getting closer to me.

George tried to convince me to fly to San Francisco with him for the weekend to get a cup of coffee and call a friend or two. I couldn't get the idea out of my head. I would have to get Joan to help cover for me. She would think it was a crazy idea, but she would help. If I got back-to-back days off and left right after work and returned in time for my shift, no one would miss me. It was such a wild idea it just might work. In the end, my good sense told me not to risk court martial for a goof.

Back Wards

Another corpsman replaced Charlie on peds. He was a lifer but only a specialist fourth class. He kept getting busted for drunkenness. He proudly showed me the photos of his children from all over the world—at least fifteen of them. It looked like a UN gathering. Half joking, half disgusted, I asked him where his Vietnamese baby was. He told me he was working on it. Clyde, another corpsman, came onto the pediatric unit. He was the worst of all and a bigot to boot. He hated peds, the children, and working with a woman.

I was being rotated more frequently as there were more wounded GIs. It was then that I met Johnny, a young, likable GI with minor frag wounds. He hailed from somewhere in the Midwest. He was a tall, good-looking farm kid who must have been around eighteen. He had received a Purple Heart for his wounds and wore it proudly pinned to his blue pajamas. He was ambulatory and helped the guys who weren't. He gave them potable water to drink, brought them urinals, and did whatever he could to help. He really was a help, especially when we were short-handed. After a couple of weeks, Johnny went back to his unit, but I would see him again.

Working on different wards, I saw all kinds of exotic diseases. The GIs cried in pain from the rabies injections of meds into their abdomens. While being debrided, a man with leprosy lost his toe. There were rumors that men with incurable syphilis were sent to a camp of no return.

Frisbee was a psychiatrist assigned to the 91st. No one could stand him, even though he was one of the most sensitive and perceptive people I met in Vietnam. In a place where so many had physical wounds, the staff did not want him uncovering our psychological wounds.

The Typhoon

Sue, the head nurse, left, and Snowflake arrived. We called her that because of her white hair and because she was an oddball. After an unsuccessful trial as a nursing supervisor, she became head nurse on pediatrics. I hated working with her and requested a transfer to any other unit. Carlos was the new corpsman on the peds unit. He was Puerto Rican, from New York, seventeen, and knew less about the world than I did. No one could take Charlie's place, but Carlos was a good corpsman and an asset to the now flakey unit.

One day when I was working with Carlos, a typhoon hit the base. At first it seemed like any other rainstorm. We thought our overhanging roof would prevent water from coming in through the burlap windows. The wind increased, and the rain began pouring in. We didn't have much rubber or waterproof material around, but whatever we had we wrapped around the children's casts and dressings. We pushed the cots close to the wall to give the children as much protection from the rain as we could. Although we put every blanket we had around them, they were still shivering with cold.

Suddenly we heard a gigantic noise and saw the

roof fly off the hooch next to us. We heard similar sounds as the corner of our roof began to go. Carlos and I ran outside. I handed sandbags to him, and he heaved them up with all his might. The sandbags seemed to hold down the roof, but some water got in, and we were all muddy and drenched. The kids were cold, wet, and scared. Some had crawled into bed with others for comfort and warmth.

As the storm started to wane, I told the corpsman to go to the mess hall next door and get a coffee urn and a big bag of coffee, paper cups, sugar, and powdered milk. While I changed dressings and tried to make the shivering children more comfortable, Carlos tried to make coffee. He had never made coffee before and dumped perhaps five pounds into the pot. It was undrinkable and grounds were everywhere. We had a good laugh. He took the pot outside and rinsed it out. Then I showed him how much coffee to put in the pot. To make it more drinkable, we added about a teaspoon or two of powdered milk and maybe ten teaspoons of sugar per cup and gave it to the children. They loved the sweet taste and the warmth.

Soon after, the unit commander came around to see how the staff and patients had fared. He asked what the kids were drinking, and when I told him, he said, "Lieutenant, don't you know that coffee isn't good for kids?"

Enraged, I lost it.

"There are a lot of things that aren't good for kids! Wars. Losing an arm, eye, or part of a leg. Losing your parents, your village, and everything you've ever known!"

I paused, and he said, "Carry on, Lieutenant" and left before he had no choice but to give me an Article 15.

SUSAN HUNT BABINSKI

Outside of Heaven

R & R CAME JUST IN TIME to keep me from going over the edge. Joan and I went together to Bangkok. To be away from the war was a luxury. Exotic temples with Buddhist monks dressed in orange surrounded us. But food, pampering, and play seemed much more important than sightseeing. For six months, I had had nothing to spend my money on, and now I was able to buy lavish presents for my family and boyfriends back home. These were the best presents I had ever bought. I drank gallons of whole milk and ate tubs of ice cream; had manicures, pedicures, and bubble baths; had my hair frosted; and went nightclubbing with every available GI. While drinking and dancing, I could forget that a few days earlier I had been trying to patch up broken bodies. Now I was just a tourist. I knew it was a fantasy, and I never allowed myself to feel that I didn't want to go back. That would have been too easy. Most AWOLs seemed to happen after a week of R & R.

Early Christmas morning, Joan and I arrived back at the 91st. Jerry and Jimmy met us at the chopper and convinced us to play Santa Claus with them and make a drop off of supplies and goodies at a Vietnamese refugee camp. That way we could extend our vacation just a few more hours. Within fifteen minutes, we were strapped in and flying off for an unauthorized afternoon's adventure.

Back on duty, eating our Christmas dinner, we heard that the cease fire for the holiday, which had been agreed to by both sides, had been broken. A young American GI was hit by a grenade while sitting on the latrine with his pants down. The doctor signed the death certificate December 26, 1967, muttering, "No one dies on Christmas."

Later, a corpsman said, "You can't even go to the can around here in peace!" We all cracked up laughing. The doctor's and corpsman's remarks spread throughout the compound.

I was now working on the back ward, and that was where I took care of Johnny again. This time he had an arm wound that was nastier and more infected than his last injury, but it healed quickly.

Looking older, Johnny seemed pleased to see me and was just as chatty and friendly as ever. Once again, he was so helpful with the other patients, both GIs and Vietnamese. The brass from his unit came around and pinned another Purple Heart and a Bronze Star on his blue pajamas. He was becoming a regular war hero and couldn't keep the grin off his face.

Over time, Johnny shared more with me about his background and how much he missed his folks. Touching his Purple Hearts, he spoke of how proud his parents were going to be of his medals. I nodded and put my hand gently on his arm. His enthusiasm brought a smile to my face.

Tom, the officer of the day, always wore his flak jacket when he made the rounds of the units and stopped to chat. One day, he showed me an excerpt from C. S. Lewis's *The Four Loves*. It held an important message for me if I was to survive Nam intact. My inner and outer lives were in such disorder.

> *To love at all is to be vulnerable. Love anything, and your heart will certainly be wrung and possibly broken. If you want to be sure of keeping it intact, you must give your heart to no one, not even an animal. Wrap it carefully around with hobbies and little luxuries; avoid all entanglements; lock it up safe in the casket or coffin of your selfishness.*

But in the casket—safe, dark, motionless, airless—it will change. It will not be broken; it will become unbreakable, impenetrable, irredeemable. The alternative to tragedy or at least the risk of tragedy is damnation. The only place outside Heaven where you can be perfectly safe from all the dangers and perturbations of love is Hell.

I made a copy of the quotation and put it in my safe/medicine cabinet. Had I learned to protect myself and my feelings in this nightmare place? Had I closed down? Could I still feel anything? I didn't know.

Since leaving Nam many years ago, I have always carried a copy of this message in my wallet as a reminder that if I got too self-involved, I would no longer be able to love.

Transition

My head nurse, Sue, finished her overseas tour and left. I could not stand working under her replacement, a major who was into army regulations and military hierarchy. At the time, I convinced myself it was because of this woman that I wanted out of my beloved pediatrics. But it was more than that. With my new understanding of my role in the war, the traumatized children, the destruction of Kim's village, I could not bear it. It was too painful, with too many losses on too many levels—I just wanted out. By then I had been in Nam seven or eight months of my year's tour. I asked to be transferred to a different unit, and the brass obliged me. My transfer came through when I got back from Bangkok, and I was sent to the PreOp/PostOp unit.

Lock Up Your Heart

The PreOp/PostOp unit was a much more hectic world than pediatrics. The ward was filled with fresh casualties and seriously injured soldiers. As the war was ramping up, there were ever more casualties. Some of the GIs were young enough to be taken into pediatric units in the States.

I liked working here. There was a lot to do. I had to keep an eye on the patients because their conditions were unstable. I often prepped patients for surgery, shaving their body hair, but sometimes they went straight into surgery. The unit was like a steel barrel cut in half with no windows and connected directly to the ER and OR. It was air-conditioned and fitted out with acute care equipment. IVs were everywhere. There were fewer patients but many more corpsmen, an extra nurse, a great deal more in and out traffic. The unit had a flushing toilet near the OR that people from all over the hospital used.

A GI in his early twenties had lost both legs above the knees and slept most of the time. We found it difficult to speak to him and were glad he slept. After several days, his doctor came in and asked me to help change the bandages. The doctor worked very gently. The blood-soaked bandages were sticking, and we used sterile water to ease them off. The GI began to scream as though he were in agony. The unit resounded with his anguish. His face was contorted in pain. His screams went through me, and I could hardly pour the water on the gauze sticking to the naked, raw, red stumps.

I implored the doctor to give him some pain medication. The doctor, still hunched over those accusing stumps, kept working without reply. He lay some instruments on a sterile towel on the bed. I suppressed the urge to move them. It was crazy, but I felt furious that he had laid his instruments where the GI's legs should have been. The GI kept screaming. I wanted to scream too. I begged the doctor to give him something. Demerol, morphine, something for God's sake. The doctor turned to me, angry.

"Don't you get it? Damn it. He is not experiencing physical pain. We have no medicine to stop this kind of pain."

I felt as if my legs had been torn out from under

me. I held on to the bed so I wouldn't fall. The GI was medevacked to Japan.

Billy

One GI named Billy had caught a frag that severed both his femoral arteries. He had been operated on to repair the arteries and was brought to the recovery room. His sutures began to hemorrhage, and he was brought back to the OR, where the doctors were able to stop the bleeding and fix both arteries. Eventually, he was brought to PostOp with both legs still attached. His legs remained icy cold, blotchy, and white, and he was routinely being given blood and intravenous fluids.

His legs stayed cold and mottled. Most of the doctors and nurses could not get a pedal pulse, but I could feel one. At first the doctors thought it was my own pulse, but it was a slower rate than mine. Billy was young and friendly and liked to talk with all the staff. He was already making plans for returning stateside and talked about how much he was looking forward to going home and seeing his family. I was giving out meds when Billy screamed, and I saw his bed filling with blood. I had the corpsman raise the foot of the bed so that Billy's legs were up high. Then I took a blood pressure cuff and put it around the bag of blood to squeeze it into him faster. I told one of the corpsmen to call the nursing supervisor, tell her the name of Billy's doctor, and explain that we had a medical emergency, then call the operating room to let them know Billy would be coming back. The blood was soon gone. I had someone put pressure on Billy's leg and gave the empty bag to the corpsman and told him to run to the lab and get more blood before it was even ordered. I opened the IV wider so he could still get fluids.

Billy looked at us with such love and comfort as though he knew he was safe. Nothing would happen because he was with us. I smiled and calmly reassured him even though I thought at the very least he was going to lose his legs. He trusted us so much. Some doctors thought he should be amputated before he went into shock. Each time he went to the OR we didn't know if he would come back with legs or not. When he returned from the OR for the third time, we saw his cold, blue legs still attached. Van, the corpsman, a conscientious objector and a Quaker, impulsively dropped to one knee and stretched his arms out to us and asked me, another nurse, and a corpsman to join him in prayer. We all knelt on one knee and held hands in the middle of the unit floor while Van asked God to allow this soldier to keep his legs. I had never experienced anything like it. We all became one person, held together as if by electricity, begging God to save one man's legs. When we stood, no one spoke. We all understood that something important had happened. Billy kept his legs. I doubt he ever knew how close he had been to losing them.

Periodically, movie stars and politicians came through the hospital to help boost morale. Once they sent a Korean veteran who was a bilateral amputee above both knees. He walked well, could run, and even did a jig for us. But we didn't want him there showing us how wonderful it was to have no legs.

Saving a Face

One young Vietnamese woman had her face blown off—no nose, no jaw, no lips, no eyebrows. There were holes where her sunken but still functioning eyes were located, holes where her nasal passages, mouth, and one ear had been. GIs would come when her dressings were being changed and asked to be allowed to take pictures of No Face. They were angry when we said no and told them she had a right to privacy. Perhaps they wanted people back home to understand that they had seen a lot of horror in the field.

Over a few months, the plastic surgeons borrowed skin, bones, and hair from other parts of her body and patched together a face for her. They made her a nose, took a bone from her leg for her jaw, took hairs from the nape of her neck to make eyebrows, and used slivers of her tongue to make lips. Her hair grew and covered the space of the missing ear. We all felt pleased with the results.

One day the *mamasan* on PreOp/PostOp ran in to get me while I was mixing IV meds. She brought me outside the unit, where the young woman with the patched-together face sat hunched over the ground, moaning and rocking back and forth holding her head. The *mamasan* kept pointing and saying, "*Dinky dow, dinky dow.*" I went over to the girl and put my hand on her shoulder and looked down to realize that she had a mirror on the ground between her legs. I couldn't say a word. The masterful work of the plastic surgeons had created a face, which though recognizably human, was still monstrous.

Colonel Graham

Colonel Skodova was replaced by Lieutenant Colonel Annie Ruth Graham. She seemed less interested in rules and regulations and more interested in nursing care and the safety and well-being of her nurses. I came to know her because she would stop by the unit to chat. She was from the hills of North Carolina and wanted to return there and buy a small farm. The army had persuaded her to take one more billet because they were short of hospital chief nurses in Nam.

One night, Colonel Graham made an unexpected visit to the PreOp unit at 4 am. She mentioned something about boots, and I got nervous. An hour earlier, I had persuaded an exhausted corpsman who had had a double shift doing guard duty to take a nap. He was asleep under light covers in a spare bed with his boots sticking out, so you could see he was not a patient. I thought she was referring to the corpsman and didn't know what to do. Recently, we had had a Korean soldier patient who had shot and nearly killed himself because he had been caught sleeping on guard duty. We resuscitated him twice. Each time, he looked angrily at us and died again. On the third try, he won. I thought about this as I stopped giving her the unit report and nervously looked over at the corpsman's boots.

But Colonel Graham pointed to her own feet. She said she knew now why her feet hurt. She had put her boots on in the dark, and they were on the wrong feet. She showed me and giggled. I was so relieved that I burst into belly laughs, and she did too. After that, I liked her even more.

One day, as I was standing outside, the Colonel noticed me without my fatigue cap. I hated it because it was hot and unattractive, but she gently insisted I put it on. I was nodding and reaching into my pocket for the cap when suddenly I heard a shrill young voice: "Susie, Susie. It's me. Chubby Bunny!" And sure enough, Chubby Bunny was running down the ramp to me, babbling away a mile a minute and pointing to herself saying, "Chubby Bunny. Chubby Bunny." Only she wasn't chubby anymore.

When Colonel Graham saw this child's excitement, she looked at me, looked at Chubby Bunny, and said, "Carry on." She quickly turned away but not quickly enough to hide the smile on her face.

Chubby Bunny hugged me and told me she had come back for some surgery. She stayed a few weeks, and I visited her now and then, but the war was escalating, and we had no time for singing songs.

Monsoon Madness

In late January, it seemed as if the monsoon would never stop. The wind blew all the time, and I wondered if we were in the middle of C. S. Lewis's hell —beyond feeling.

A sweet-faced GI who did not look dead was brought into the ER while I was packing up supplies.

He must have been all of seventeen or eighteen years old. He was slim and blond and looked like a child. He looked so healthy, without the usual blood and guts spilling out. He looked more asleep than dead, but he was dead. We tried to resuscitate him without success, at first gently, then vigorously when he didn't respond. We looked all over his body for some clue to his death but came up with nothing. I felt angry because I couldn't understand what had happened to him. Finally, we saw it, a tiny black mole-like frag spot no bigger than a pinpoint on the left side of his chest just below the heart. It seemed so unbelievable that something so tiny could kill a person.

We called the graves unit, but they didn't answer the phone. They were busy. Too many young men were being packed up to be shipped home, their tour permanently over. A couple of young corpsmen ran to get a body bag. None of us could stand to leave him under a sheet. He was too close to us all and had to be taken out of the ER as quickly as possible.

The corpsmen returned with the olive drab bag. We noticed a name tag attached, but there was no body inside. A corpsman opened the bag and felt inside. He shouted, "There's something in there!" He pulled out a charred foot. That was all that was left of nineteen-year-old PFC William Scott. We all laughed hysterically until we collapsed sobbing. William Scott would go home in a sealed coffin. How awful it would be if someone opened the coffin and found nothing but a foot.

By late January, things were hectic. Choppers were continually flying in and out with fresh casualties. While picking up a patient in the ER to transfer to PreOp, I recognized a young lieutenant from the officers club. He ran toward the gurney which held his captain, a man in his thirties, whom I had also met at the club. As he reached the gurney, the lieutenant realized the man's head was not fully attached to his body. Holding his own head, he ran out screaming. I realized when he screamed that I was feeling nothing at all. I wondered for a moment why I did not react more. I told myself I didn't have time. I had work to do.

Photos and Flowers

I went along with Dave, a medical doctor I was dating, on a sanctioned MEDCAP (Medical Civic Action Program) trip to Cum Sung, a Montagnard village about thirty-five miles inland near a Green Beret camp. MEDCAP was a program developed by the US military to give medical aid to the people of Vietnam. With its lights off, under cover of darkness, our chopper flew into the mountains. As we walked into the village, the little children looked so cute running around naked, smoking pot pipes. As soon as the villagers saw our chopper with the red cross, they began to cough. It turned out that the Vietnamese liked the taste of cough medicine, and so they would line up for sick call and were given one teaspoon each. I'm not sure how much medical help we gave these people, but it created positive American propaganda. I loved the whole experience. We took Polaroid pictures of some of the children and adults and showed the photos to them. At first, they were frightened because they didn't understand what they were seeing. They thought we had taken their spirits. To try to explain, we traced their outlines on the ground and pointed to them. They seemed to understand. When we gave them the photos, they were happy again.

On the mission, we visited a nearby Special Forces camp surrounded by beautiful yellow flowering plants, the first flowers I had seen in months. I told Dave how much I missed flowers. He understood. He suggested we dig one up and bring it back to the 91st.

We flew out in the helicopter under cover of darkness with no lights on. Soon there was trouble. We heard shots and saw red tracer bullets aimed at us. I didn't know in advance about tracer bullets but understood instantly. About every fifth bullet was a tracer so that sights could be adjusted. Strapped in one side of the helicopter, I watched the endless progression of red bullets arcing toward us. All I could do was grit my teeth and think, *You missed, you idiot! You missed!*

Luckily, we made it back safely. Later, we heard that the helicopter *had* been hit, more than once, but nothing vital had been damaged.

The day after Dave and I got back to the base, we dug a hole and planted the yellow flower in front of my sleeping quarters. I was teased about being like Lady Bird Johnson, beautifying the compound. The plant looked odd sticking out of the sand in front of my hooch, but I loved it.

Sometimes when I was on night duty, Colonel Graham made the rounds, and we'd chat a bit. She told me that Vietnam would be her last tour. She planned to return to the hills of North Carolina and plant a garden. She loved seeing things grow.

Losing Johnny

It was around this time that I saw Johnny again, the boy hero with all the medals whom I had nursed twice before on the back ramp. Purple Hearted Johnny whom nothing could kill. I ran over and knelt beside him and tried to talk to him. He murmured a little sound but didn't respond after that. Instead, he just had an empty stare.

I was very upset. The staff reassured me that his wound wasn't so bad. He'd make it. And now he would have a third Purple Heart. I shook my head. I was exhausted and just wanted to sleep. I told people on the unit he was dying, but no one else could see it. His bleeding was under control, but I knew the spark of life was gone. His eyes were dead.

The next night, Dave came to walk me home from duty. I was pleased, but I asked him why. He had never done that before. He told me Joan was worried about me, and then he told me that Johnny had died. The doctors said it was pneumonia, but I knew that just finished the job. Too many bullets, too much pain, too many buddies killed, too many babies burned—that was what really killed him. He was already dead when we got him.

I lost it. I believe it was the only time I cried in Nam. Without a word, Dave just held me, and I cried and cried. During my year in Vietnam I learned the power of two people touching or sharing hugs when words seemed empty or just created more distance. To be held and to feel the warmth and comfort of another person meant so much there. While the flower children chanted, "Make love not war," many nurses, including me, felt guilty for not measuring up to our own moral standards for what a good girl should or should not feel, think, or do. How sad that we bear the guilt for being human.

After Johnny died, I was really down, and then a minor miracle happened. I had neither the energy nor the will to water my much-loved yellow flower. And yet it survived and looked beautiful. I thought about it during my long workdays and felt renewed every night after seeing it. Months later, I learned from one of the nurses that Colonel Graham had been lugging a pail over and watering the plant daily. I believe she saved more than the flower.

That was her last garden. She died of a stroke before her tour ended, the highest-ranking American servicewoman to die in Vietnam.

The Wave

It was not just one incident that caused our moment of despair and madness. Perhaps it was the accumulation of having seen too much too often. One night after work, I met Joan, who suggested we go to the officers club. I was tired but agreed. A lot of men we had never seen before were there. I drank my usual Scotch and soda. After a while, two young officers joined us, and one of them suggested going for a walk along the beach. It was during the monsoon season, and the sea was exceptionally dramatic. The waves must have been ten or fifteen feet high. The currents were so strong we had been warned not to go in even ankle deep because we could be swept out to sea. We heard that two troopers from a nearby unit had been drowned. The night was dark except for the light from the stars. The thunderous roar of the crashing waves prevented any conversation. We all just stood there. I was mesmerized as I gazed into the semi-darkness.

Without a word, one of the officers and I joined hands and ran into the swelling sea. I was calm as the cold water poured over us and grabbed us and started pulling us out to sea. The only warmth I felt was the tight grip of the officer's hand on my hand and wrist. Everything was heightened, and as I felt stones trickling down my fatigue shirt, I knew with calm acceptance and no remorse that we were going to drown. I did not struggle. I just waited patiently. Thank God, the officer had a tight grip on my wrist. Suddenly a huge wave tossed us back onto the shore. In the aftershock of nearly dying, Joan and I regained our senses and left our escorts behind. We never saw them again. I wonder how many accidents in Nam were really acts of despair and madness.

SUSAN HUNT BABINSKI

There and Here

THE TET OFFENSIVE was launched on January 31, 1968. More than one hundred cities and towns in South Vietnam were attacked by the Viet Cong and the North Vietnamese military troops. There was a shortage of nurses at the hospital, and the younger nurses were sometimes sent to units other than their assigned ones. I was sent to the women's unit, and over time, to most of the back units. That included the prisoner of war unit surrounded by barbed wire, with locked doors and guards out front. I made it clear to a staff member who hinted that prisoner patients didn't deserve such good care that I would tolerate nothing but the best for them. Although prisoners, these patients were often teenagers or young adults who didn't seem like enemies to me. They were the same age as my South Vietnamese patients and looked like them. Once I saw a female patient, a Viet Cong nurse. She kept looking at me as I did at her. We could just as easily have been in each other's place.

On one shift, I put lotion on an old Vietnamese *papasan*. He was ill, but I don't think he was actively dying. His eyes spoke of an overwhelming sadness. As I rubbed his thin frame with lotion and spoke to him in a soothing tone, he seemed pleased. He didn't have a clue as to what I was saying, but he seemed thankful that I was being kind and gentle. In some way, I was paying tribute to my grandfather in the States. I had learned of my grandfather's recent death in a letter from my mother.

Litters lined up outside the hospital. Tuy Hòa had been hit, so we took soldiers, children, civilians, everyone. I was so tired I wanted to lie down, and when I finally did, I wanted to burst out crying, but I was so tired I couldn't cry. As terrible as it was, I felt good about what I was doing. I have never felt so needed as I was then.

The rain began to subside. Our mad dash into the sea still scared me and put me back in touch with reality.

The New Routine

Once Tet began, we could no longer hold walk-in

clinics in towns beyond the base. Many GIs were sent to the 91st with minor wounds before being sent back into battle. Sometimes we stabilized the seriously ill men before sending them to Saigon or directly out of the country to China, Japan, or Hawaii for more extensive care. Under less warlike conditions, I was told that occasionally and unbeknownst to the GI, his temperature would be quietly fudged to keep him in the hospital because he was so close to the end of his duty assignment when he would be returning to the States. I also heard that some young GIs didn't want to go home but wanted to return to the field to help their buddies.

As the fighting intensified, our hours increased from eight- to twelve-hour shifts six days a week. Many of the casualties being brought in needed immediate surgery if they were to survive. When we were technically off duty, we would often help by washing surgical instruments before they were sterilized, restocking supplies, preparing IVs to be hung—doing whatever was needed on the units.

Sometimes the staff worked such long hours that they fell asleep while caring for a patient. I saw a corpsman taking a patient's blood pressure fall asleep on his feet and topple over. Fortunately, he hit the bed but not the patient, which cushioned his fall to the cement floor, so he was not seriously hurt. I heard him say he had been working almost twenty-four hours. I told him to take a nap.

Jerry Goes MIA

I used to love the whirring sound of a chopper. My adrenaline began to flow when I heard that sound. Now, whenever I hear a helicopter overhead, I have a wrenching physical reaction. Sometimes before I am conscious of it, my body responds, and I feel an overwhelming sadness. It is because of my memory of the injured but especially because of Jerry.

On February 11, four days before my twenty-third birthday, I was on duty when I got word that three choppers had gone down. Jerry was piloting one of them. Word spread quickly throughout the 91st when Jerry and his crew did not return from picking up casualties. I knew he was scheduled to go to Hawaii soon to meet his wife for R & R. All that day, I waited to hear the choppers returning, but that sound never came. When I first heard they were MIA, I was devastated but unable to cry. Tears would mean acknowledging that they were dead, and the thought was more than I could bear. Every time I heard a chopper, I prayed it was them, but it never was.

For the first time, I felt hatred toward the

Vietnamese. Only the children escaped my anger. My hatred did not last long, but I was suspicious of the Vietnamese and more cautious around them. For several weeks, Joan and I hung around the chopper unit dispatch tent, hoping to hear some good news, but Jerry and the others remained MIA. He was the second friend the army took from me—the first by orders, the second by death.

I loved Jerry, but I knew he was married and that he loved his wife. He was only mine for such a short time. He was so sweet and gentle, and he listened when I told him about Kim and her destroyed village. Although I went out with many men in Vietnam, I didn't allow myself to get too attached so that I wouldn't miss them after they left. When my friends from those days ask me which of my men friends I cared for the most, the truthful answer is Jerry. I still miss him so.

Everything Hits the Fan

When we had many casualties with severe injuries, the doctors would triage. That meant separating out for treatment those who had the best chance of survival from those with little hope. No one talked about it much. The doctors made the decisions. I realized that triage was not only about survival risks, for rarely was a GI triaged to die, but suspected VC and NVA often were. When the soldiers were unconscious, it didn't bother me so much, but it did when they were half-awake. One GI kept gesturing that he had to get to surgery fast. I soothed him and told him to save his strength, to close his eyes and rest, knowing when he gave up the struggle he would die. The only thing keeping him alive was his young body and desperate will to live.

I can recall the terrible sounds of soldiers triaged to die. One ARVN soldier, considered too far gone to operate on, kept choking on his own secretions. He kept trying to get our attention to help him, to suction him. He didn't know he was supposed to die. He might have died sooner if I had not suctioned him, but I couldn't stand his gurgling protests. I didn't think it was right that he should die in his own secretions. I could hear his gurgle everywhere I went on the unit. I suctioned him to give myself peace of mind and him a few more minutes of life.

The doctor was working to get people ready for surgery. A baby, maybe four or five months old, had been triaged to die as there was no surgery that could help. The baby began to cry. I couldn't bear it and walked over and picked the baby up from the plastic bed box and talked softly and gently while walking back and forth. The baby stopped crying and looked peaceful. The doctor became angry and said we had to work with those we could help. I understood but added that we did help the baby, as the baby was no longer crying. Looking around the room, I realized there were fewer tears and less groaning coming from the patients waiting to be helped. Some were smiling and nodded, clearly approving of my comforting the baby. I told the doctor that it was better than a tranquillizer, for more than just the baby. I put the infant back in her bed box and continued to help the doctor. Later, I went to check on her. She had died.

Snowflake, helping in PreOp, had to shave a GI waiting to go to surgery. I couldn't believe my eyes when I saw what she was doing. The shave was meant to prepare him for abdominal surgery, but she was carefully shaving the soldier's week-old beard. I wanted to laugh, but something stopped me. The two of them seemed so serene, untouched by the craziness around us. The GI, who a moment before looked so terrible and terrifying, so scared and scary, now looked civilized, human, and relaxed.

Another young soldier had developed a liver abscess from amoebic dysentery. His skin, eyes, and even the sheets where he lay turned golden yellow. I had never seen anything like that. When he died, the medical doctor who had cared for him for months on the IC unit openly wept as he signed the death certificate. We all had certain patients who got to us.

The Last Couple of Months

In April, Joan, our friend Phyllis, and I went to Hong Kong. Dave, who had planted the yellow flower for me, met us there. This time, I ached to go home. My tour was coming to an end, and it was painful for me to call home because I was so close to the end of my tour I could taste it.

Dave and I spent a lot of time together. We went to the top of the mountain by tram and looked down upon the city below. We ate on the huge boat restaurant in Hong Kong Harbor. We drank lots of champagne and partied all day. Dave was due to leave for home right after we returned to the base. He seemed to be getting a little serious, asking me questions like "What would you do if you were married to someone who made $50,000 a year?"

Later, back at the 91st, Dave went berserk looking for a small box he had lost in the sand in front of my hooch. He wouldn't say what it was except that it was a goodbye gift. Suddenly, I had the feeling that it was a ring. As he tore around looking for it, I half hoped he wouldn't find it. He never told me what it was. Dave's tour was over. I rode to the air force base to see him off.

Within a week, Randy, a young chopper pilot, and I became friends. He wanted a mother more than a lover. He didn't want to kiss but to be held close to my breast and have me smooth his hair while he told me about his fears. His men were angry with him because he refused to go in under heavy fire to pick up a dying GI. The medics on the ground begged him over the radio to come quickly or their friend would die. Randy's men wanted to go in, but he said no. He was not going to risk four more lives. His men called him chicken. Randy wasn't sure himself if he had done the right thing.

Dave's friend Jim complained angrily that I didn't wait long before finding someone new. I was surprised. All romances seemed so temporary in Nam that it hadn't dawned on me that I was being unfaithful to Dave.

Spring was coming, but I was drained by all the losses I had experienced. The injuries seemed to increase daily, and I was needed to patch up so many battered young men. My mind was not in Vietnam anymore. I was getting ready to return to the real world.

I decided that when I returned to the States and civilian life, I really wanted to go to a university and get a bachelor's degree in nursing and then work with inner-city children and their families in a medical intensive care unit. I discovered when applying to some universities that I could get credits for some of my nursing school courses. To get those credits, I needed to take proctored exams, and if I passed, I would receive credit and not have to repeat those courses. Major Gorman spoke with me about the process and agreed to proctor me. I took those exams in the middle of an ICU ward filled with wounded soldiers while bombs were exploding outside. I passed them, received credit for the courses, and applied for admission to several programs. Long Island University in Brooklyn, New York, accepted me and gave me a whole semester of credit as well as an additional grant. My superiors told me that if I stayed in the army, they would arrange for me to be promoted to captain. I thanked them but said no. They said I'd be sorry because a civilian job would be too boring after military life. But I had had enough of their kind of excitement.

Flying Back to the States

My orders to return to the States came before Joan's, and I was flown to Saigon under the cover of darkness. It was quiet when I boarded the Braniff Airlines flight back to the States. The plane was filled to capacity. Except for the stewardess, I was the only female on board. No alcohol was served on the flight.

At takeoff time, word spread quickly that a plane carrying returning vets had been hit and crashed into the China Sea with no survivors. It was said that the story of that crash had been kept out of the papers, covered up, because it was thought to be too demoralizing for the troops. There was an audible sigh of relief as we climbed higher. The pilot announced, "Attention everyone. We have left Vietnam." Thunderous applause and whistling broke out.

For most of the flight, the men slept. I could not, but I didn't feel like talking to the young GI next to me trying to make conversation. Many of the soldiers were young and looked as though they had come from the fields. I thought of Johnny, the sweet hero, a kid dead from pneumonia and war, and felt lucky that I had had a job I could live with. As we landed in Seattle, Washington, the pilot said, "Welcome to the World." Everyone gave a shout of joy. Many of us had tears coming down our faces. As we left the plane, some vets knelt and kissed the American soil, and some blessed themselves. Many shouted, "God bless America!" I don't think any of us realized then that just as we were coming home, many Americans were "God damning" us.

When I went to Vietnam, I was twenty-two and just out of nursing school. When I came back, I was twenty-three, with the experiences of that year forever embedded in me. It would take years before I understood how strongly I had been affected. But I never regretted my decision to go. I felt it was meant to be. Over time, I understood that I had been changed forever, in just a year.

Getting Out and Going Home

The middle-aged civilian ladies in Seattle who helped to process out those who had completed their military duty must have thought I was mad. I wanted to resign my commission on the day I returned from Vietnam because I had heard a rumor that without resigning your commission you were technically still in the service and could be recalled to duty.

My request set up a stir in the office. The white-haired woman helping me suggested that I wait and apply for my GI Bill benefits right away. I refused. She conferred with several of her colleagues, all of whom tried to convince me to wait and not resign until after my approval for GI benefits went through. I asked for absolute reassurance that no one was going to send me back to Nam. These kindly ladies reassured me that the possibility was so remote that the risk was negligible. None of them could give me the reassurance I wanted.

I ran into the restroom. All my plans seemed to be in jeopardy, and I really needed the GI Bill. They could not have known that even a negligible risk, so remote it was not worth considering, was an unbearable possibility for me. No one could give me total assurance. One woman followed me into the restroom to make sure I was not planning to kill myself. I washed my face, regained my composure, and went back out to the office. I sat down and agreed to wait a week or two, knowing that, if forced, I could always escape to Canada, where my sister and brother-in-law lived.

I had ordered a yellow Barracuda convertible while in Nam and arranged to pick up Joan, whose orders had now come through, in Seattle. She and I had already spoken about traveling across the country and seeing some friends from nursing school who had settled in California before heading back to the East Coast. A group of GIs we knew, also recently back from Vietnam, asked if they could ride to California with us. We made the trip together, singing sixties songs as we drove along. We had a great visit with our California friends and rode a trolley for the first time. Hippies were everywhere smoking pot, but we did not, though it was offered to us often. The weather was wonderful, and I loved zooming along in my convertible with the top down. I often went too fast, and Joan had to remind me to slow down. Our trip across the country took about two weeks.

When we got to Rhode Island, Joan and I decided to stop at the Howard Johnson's restaurant we used to go to when we were in nursing school. We ordered coffee milkshakes and fried onion rings—always our favorites. As we were enjoying our meal, Joan's aunt and uncle came in. They were surprised to see us and started asking about when we had gotten back. We both felt guilty when we told them we hadn't been home yet. Joan wanted to leave right after they were seated, as she knew her folks would be upset that we were five or ten minutes away and taking our time. We finished quickly, and I dropped Joan off, declining her pleas to come in with her. I felt I had to get home now, too. As I drove up to the house, I saw a big sign in the window. *Welcome Home*. There were lots of kisses and misty eyes.

Some neighbors didn't recognize me. I had lost so much weight. I also had the best tan of my life, having turned a deep mahogany by the end of my tour of duty. The next thing I did was tender my letter of resignation from the army. My second day home, I told my hometown boyfriend that I was not going to marry him and that I was heading to New York City to go to college.

I didn't talk about my Vietnam experiences when I came back. I noticed Joan did not either. I just didn't know how to begin, and, on some level, I feared being overwhelmed with intense feelings. I worried that if I allowed myself to cry, I wouldn't be able to stop. Most people did not know I was a Vietnam veteran, and I did not tell them.

After I was home a while, my father confided his earlier fears that if I went to Vietnam, I might become insensitive or even neurotic. He never shared his feelings about his time in the army in World War II. What angered me most was that after my return from Vietnam, he didn't notice that I had changed. In his eyes, I resumed being the happy, carefree daughter he had known before the war. But that was not who I was now. He would often say he was glad that I was still the same. I played a little game when talking with him on the phone. I would think of Nam and get lost in reverie until he asked, "Are you still there?" I would always tell him, "Yes, Dad, I'm still there." He never caught on that I was not saying "here" but "there."

Perhaps he didn't want to know that his little Susie had changed forever. He was a veteran. Could he not see that I would never be the person he had known before Vietnam? I never let on, just went along as if everything was fine.

After my father died, my uncle, his brother, told me of an incident from World War II that involved my father. He was an army captain stationed in France, where he and another captain were in charge of a group of GIs. There was fighting in the area, and as they approached a mountainside, they heard weapons firing and bombs exploding. My father and his fellow officer decided to split up the unit and go quietly around both sides of the mountain path to see if they could surprise the enemy. They flipped a coin to determine which direction each group would take. My father and his group ran into no one as they walked around the mountain. Then they discovered the remains of the other captain and his group. All were dead. My uncle, with tears in his eyes, said my father cried as he told the story. My father never spoke of it again with my uncle and told no one else. In tears, I nodded my understanding and wished Dad had shared that story with me.

Later that summer, I moved to Brooklyn with Joan and some other friends and rented an apartment in preparation for starting my first semester at Long Island University and a completely new life.

SUSAN HUNT BABINSKI

My Return to the World

IN THOSE EARLY MONTHS at Long Island University (LIU), I felt like a stranger in the world, but I pushed aside my confusion. My feelings were so mixed, and I did not want to explain them. I had been blown apart even though you couldn't see my wounds. In the company of others, I felt worlds away from everyone else. Sitting in a room with a group of chatting, laughing college students watching the daily television news that showed footage of Vietnam casualties was almost more than I could bear. I just sat there drinking my Coke, not saying anything, but feeling terribly sad, angry, and alone. Over time, I settled myself a little and volunteered to tutor in a reading program for inner-city children. It was about this time that I started to learn more about the protests against the war.

Messy Edges

Anti-war protests happened frequently in New York City at the time. My friends were not politically active and did not take part in anti-war marches. But I had to go. To me, the peace marches were more grueling than any military march I had been on. Despite the huge number of protesters, I always marched alone, trying to understand myself. I didn't feel self-righteous like so many of my fellow marchers. I cringed when I heard them scream "baby killers" at veterans in uniform or people with family members in Nam who would challenge them along the way. I envied them for feeling so sure they were right. But I also resented the jeering spectators who spit on us marchers and called us Commies for opposing the government. I felt utterly silent and alone.

My first year at LIU, I met a fellow vet in one of my courses. Something came up in class, and he found out I was a veteran. I hadn't said much to anyone about my war experiences since my first day back home. He hadn't either. He was a solidly built guy and patriotic down to the American flag decal on his notebook. He was older than the other students and seemed much older than his actual age.

One day after class, he began talking to me. We decided to go to Junior's restaurant, famous for its cheesecake and three-day dill pickles, across the street from the campus. He said he had been an army grunt in the jungles of Nam in an area of heavy fighting. He felt bad about much of what he had done, like shooting civilians and watching his captain intentionally get fragged by his own men for being a chicken. He was trying to justify what he had done as right under the circumstances and probably half believed what he was saying. He assumed that I agreed with him, but he didn't ask me. He just kept justifying himself. I saw that he was in a lot of pain, and his anguish ignited my own. I could empathize with him. After this conversation, I felt even more alone.

Dave, who lost the box in the sand in Vietnam, came to see me and still seemed interested in me, but I needed distance from Nam and my memories of it. We never saw each other again.

I saw Bob again, now in law school. He sensed I had changed but was unable to articulate how. He knew a few Vietnam vets in law school, some without arms or legs, but no one saw their invisible wounds.

In exchange for my youth, I gained a kind of wisdom about myself and other people. It is much easier to believe, like a child, that life and people are simple. Without messy edges. But after you have been in a war, you know that life is not neat. In Vietnam, I gained respect for the human ability not only to endure the unendurable and survive, but also to thrive.

Hugh

I met my husband, Hugh, at LIU, where he was my professor in a small English honors seminar. He had served in the navy years earlier. I felt an immediate kinship with him. He was eight years older than I, but I felt so much more comfortable with him than I did with my young classmates. He and I did not date until I was out of his class. Hugh claimed he fell in love with me when I first walked into his classroom. I am not sure when I knew that he was the one for me, but it didn't take long.

In 1970, two months before we were to be married, there was a huge women's march against the war in Washington, DC. LIU provided a bus for anyone interested in going. I told Hugh I had to go to the DC protest and that I did not want company. He understood and made no attempt to stop me. I decided not to go on the LIU bus because I didn't want to be with a bunch of college kids. Instead, I took a separate bus from the Port Authority Terminal in Manhattan. I knew the march was important, but I was conflicted and confused, as if my participating were a betrayal of my former patients and friends. In my heart, though, I knew I was doing it for them.

Liddy, who had been our protector at Fitzsimons Army Medical Center in Denver and was now making a career in the Army Nurses Corps, was stationed at Walter Reed Hospital and lived in the DC area. When I got off the bus, I took a cab and showed up unannounced on her doorstep at midnight. I told her why I was there, and she took me in. Of course, she knew all about the march. She never challenged my going but told me I had to do what I thought was right. The next day after breakfast she dropped me off where the march was forming. She was a little nervous because she was on active duty and there were cameras everywhere, reporters, and some secret service. She was afraid she might get into trouble if she were caught on videotape. I believe I needed her to say it was okay for me to participate and that it did not mean I was being disloyal to other Vietnam veterans.

Graduate Education and Work

After returning from Vietnam, I felt sure I wanted to work with children who were experiencing some kind of trauma. After I finished my undergraduate degree at Long Island University, I went to New York University to get a two-year master's degree as a clinical nurse specialist in child and adolescent psychiatric nursing. As part of my master's program, I was enrolled in a sensitivity group with other graduate school nurses run by Dr. Susan Lego. One nurse spoke with sadness about the recent loss of her dog. I felt sorry for her and then began to think of all the losses I experienced during that year in Vietnam. Dr. Lego turned to me and asked me to speak. The dam broke. I cried. I told the group about being in Vietnam, my sadness, anger, and all the losses. After that I shut down and did not speak about my experiences in Nam again for a long time.

I had been back in the States for quite a while when I received a package in the mail from the US Army. It was on a weekend, and my husband was with me when I removed the wrapping and found a handsome wooden display case. On a bed of blue velvet was an Army Commendation Medal. I looked at it for a few seconds and then went over to the trash and tossed it in. I thought of Johnny, the kids in the pediatric ward, and many others and felt like bawling. Hugh held me in his arms for several minutes before I pulled away and reminded him that we needed to get going with our chores.

Several years later, Hugh and I were at a faculty party at Columbia University, where he taught. A young assistant professor started to complain about the "crazy vets" she was getting in her classes. It must have seemed like a safe crowd to air those feelings. The people at the party were older professors, wives of faculty, single women, and youngish men with recently acquired doctorates. Some were shocked when I said quietly, "I'm a Vietnam veteran." After they got over their initial shock, a young assistant professor in the English department asked me, "What did you do there?" I told her I had been a nurse. The woman who had complained about the vets in her classes said, "Oh, that doesn't count. You're not really a vet."

I didn't say another word. But later I started to question myself. Was I really a Vietnam veteran? It took me a long time to answer this question. We nurses saw and cared for more damaged bodies than the soldiers in the field. In the chaos of battle, they often had little time to feel all their emotions. Nurses could not escape from the pain and suffering we saw every day. Eventually, I was able to feel that, yes, without any qualifiers, I am truly a Vietnam veteran.

Children's Lives

After finishing my master's degree at NYU, I qualified as a child and adolescent psychiatric nurse. While I was in graduate school, I joined with some other nurse volunteers to set up a Child Life Program that provided emotional care for often gravely ill, inner-city children and their families. I decided I needed more mental health experience before returning to a pediatric setting. The director of the Bronx Children's Psychiatric Center hired me. The children we saw were mainly from minority families in the South Bronx, and many of them had been traumatized. Some had been sexually and physically abused. Many suffered from minor mental illness. Parental abandonment through illness, drugs, or imprisonment was not uncommon. Entire families were sometimes wiped out by AIDS. Some of the teenagers had been HIV positive since birth. For the first time since leaving pediatrics in Vietnam, I felt at home. I belonged here.

At the Children's Psychiatric Center, I chose to work in day care as I felt the children should be kept at home with their families if possible. I often made home visits even though in the 1970s the South Bronx was considered dangerous because of the drugs and violence. I felt that what I did mattered and that I could be of help to these kids and their families. And in a very real way, they helped me too. Was this a continuation of my life in Vietnam? In some ways, yes. But I loved my work, and looking back, I believe it allowed me to have a life at a time when I was still trying to heal from the war.

Numbered Lives

I stayed at Bronx Children's for twenty-eight years. During the time that I was working in the Bronx, I returned to New York University to get a PhD in psychology. From the beginning, I knew that I wanted to study the experiences of women nurses who served in Vietnam. While working on my master's degree in child and adolescent psychiatric nursing at NYU, I had participated in several studies about women nurses who had served in Vietnam. These studies enrolled as many nurses as possible, aiming for a large N (number of participants), and used statistically based methods, relying on surveys that could be completed quickly. They all wanted me to rate my experiences from one to five.

This approach was incredibly frustrating to me. How do you rate nursing a soldier with his legs blown off on a Likert scale from one to five? What number should you use to describe how you felt while holding a tiny baby who had just been orphaned when her whole village was destroyed in a bombing raid? Is five a high enough rating for how it felt to go up with a pilot on a supply mission, skimming over the edge of the China Sea while red tracer bullets were lighting up the sky all around you?

Waiting to Weep

I wanted to study the experience of nurses in Vietnam on a much deeper level, using qualitative research methods to study a small number of women who had served as nurses in Vietnam, interviewing them at length about their experiences during the war and their lives in the States since returning.

Fortunately, I was able to find three NYU professors who strongly supported the kind of research I wanted to do: Ester Buchholz, my chairperson; Margot Ely; and Jim Hinojosa. Using my connections with various organizations for veterans or nurses, I recruited a small number of women who agreed to participate in my study. I made it clear to them that they could drop out at any time if they began to feel uncomfortable. I also assured them that their identities would be disguised in the dissertation.

Professor Margot Ely, who specialized in qualitative research, recommended I join a writing support group to meet with regularly during the dissertation process. In 1990, I formed a group with three women I had met in one of my doctoral courses. Jane Isenberg, Pat Juell, and Rebecca Mlynarczyk were all working on doctorates in English education. I was the only one in psychology. Despite our different research specialties, our group really worked for us. We met monthly to discuss our writing throughout the dissertation process and for many years after that as we pursued new writing projects.

While I was working on my dissertation, my chairperson, Ester Buchholz, recommended that I read extensively about post-traumatic stress disorder (PTSD), which would inform my understanding of the experiences the nurses shared with me. As I did this reading, I realized that undertaking this dissertation topic was surely a continuation of my attempt to come to terms with my own Vietnam experiences.

One of the most common symptoms of PTSD

is recurring, terrifying nightmares about wartime experiences. When I first returned to the States, I did have a few nightmares, but I could no longer remember what they were about. In fact, I even forgot that I had had any frightening dreams until a friend reminded me years later. I do remember staying away from movies and TV shows about the war. I understand now that I didn't want any triggers to set me off. Friends told me about the TV show *M*A*S*H*, set in Korea, but really about Vietnam. They said it was amusing and urged me to see it. They didn't understand that I wasn't worried about seeing what was shown on TV but instead about what it might trip in me.

When I finally did see films about Vietnam, I didn't suffer any nightmares, but I felt infinitely sad. Only in 1996, when I saw *The English Patient*, set in World War II, did I have a series of nightmares. In one I was being raped. What today is viewed as sexual harassment was common in the 1960s, but in those days many of us thought that's just how it was between the sexes. I was never assaulted in Vietnam except for an occasional unwanted kiss. I wasn't raped, but a psychologist friend suggested that perhaps my dream reflected my experience of what happened to me psychically in Nam. Another nightmare triggered by the same film featured a young GI who had all his fingers blown off, and I was responsible. I woke up feeling ashamed, horrified, and convinced I was crazy. I can't describe the feeling I had inside, but the dream left me shaking horribly and feeling physically ill.

Several of the nurses I interviewed told me they had suffered from recurring nightmares for years after returning from Vietnam. But that did not stop them from moving on with their lives. Most of them had been very successful in their chosen careers. Some had struggled with multiple relationships. Others had remained single. All felt their lives had been forever changed by their wartime experiences. And all of them felt that the wartime experiences of women nurses who served in Vietnam were not getting the same kind of respect and attention as those of the men who served on the battlefields. They felt that they were the invisible veterans, and one of their reasons for volunteering for my study was the hope that this would bring more attention to the role that women had played in the war.

My research participants and I knew about the efforts to erect a statue on the National Mall in Washington to honor the sacrifices of women veterans of the Vietnam War. The dedication of this statue in 1993 was so important to all of us because at last there was a public acknowledgment of the important roles we had played in the war.

It even inspired the title for my dissertation, which I completed in 1996: "Did We Have to Wait Twenty-Five Years to Weep in Front of a Monument? A Qualitative Study of Six Women Vietnam Veteran Nurses."

Monuments and Memories

THE VIETNAM VETERANS Memorial Wall, designed by Yale undergraduate Maya Lin, was dedicated on November 13, 1982. At that time, it listed 57,939 names of those who died in the war, arranged by date of death. This list included Colonel Annie Graham, my beloved nursing supervisor, who had watered my yellow flower when I was too tired and discouraged to do it myself. Colonel Graham died of medical complications in August 1968 while still in Vietnam. Approximately 1,300 MIA/POWs were also listed on the Wall. Jerry was one of them.

On November 11, 1984, The Three Soldiers, a statue honoring the GIs who served in Vietnam, was dedicated near the Wall.

Dedication of the Vietnam Women's Memorial

We nurses were very supportive of these memorials, which had been given a place of honor on the National Mall in Washington. But we felt our own sacrifices were being ignored. Compared with the three million men who served in Vietnam, women were a relatively small number—more than ten thousand, approximately ninety percent of whom were nurses. The fact that no one had thought to honor them with their own monument pointed clearly to how women were treated in the military in those years and, for that matter, in society at large. Women were seen as handmaidens to the doctors and helpmates to their husbands. Men were considered stronger, more independent, and unemotional. Women were considered weaker, dependent on men, and unable to control their emotions.

In 1984, Diane Carlson, a nurse veteran herself, founded the Vietnam Women's Memorial Project and worked tirelessly to raise money for a memorial for all women who served in Vietnam. Glenna Goodacre designed a statue of three women in uniform tending to a wounded soldier. On November 11, 1993, nine years after the men's statue was installed, the Vietnam Women's Memorial was dedicated. This was the first monument ever to acknowledge American women who served abroad during wartime.

I attended the dedication of the Women's Memorial and saw many old friends from Nam for the first time since I left in 1968. Many former patients as well as other soldiers came to the dedication to support the women veterans. One man in a motorized wheelchair with both legs missing and his face badly scarred came up to Liddy, Joan, and me along with his lovely wife. He said, "I came here today because I want to say thank you to all the nurses who served in Nam for being there for me and the other guys. I'm glad to be alive." In tears, I thanked him and gave him a long hug. He returned the hug and said, "Welcome home." At that moment, I felt both proud and sad to be a veteran.

I have always had a close bond with other women who served in Vietnam. At the dedication of the women's statue, we felt that our service was finally being honored. We cried, hugged, and told stories that some had never until that moment shared with anyone. I looked forward to seeing my head nurse from pediatrics, Captain Sue, my role model, who had been so good with the children. Instead, there was a letter saying how proud she was of the statue and how sad she was because she couldn't be there. Several months before the dedication, she died of pancreatic cancer.

While attending the dedication ceremonies, I learned for the first time that Tuy Hòa and the 91st had been declared Agent Orange centers. Everyone who worked there had been exposed. I was shocked to learn of the terrible effects of this chemical. I don't know how I would have reacted if I had known all those cleft palates and the physical, mental, and developmental deformities I saw on the pediatrics unit were the result of the use of Agent Orange as a defoliant. Many of the nurses at the dedication spoke through tears about having had or currently having cancers—all connected to Agent Orange. Others spoke of staff who had died young of cancer. A fair number in our small group spoke of giving birth to developmentally delayed or disabled children. Some still suffered from amoebic dysentery as well as what was called the Vietnamese Time Bomb, a serious pneumonia that often developed years after a person was originally infected. There are no Purple Hearts for medical illnesses.

Survivor guilt is often discussed, but I think many people do not fully understand its implications. I call it the dirty little secret that survivors know. People younger and smarter than you, better human beings than you, have died, and you have been given the gift of life. Many of the women who gathered for the dedication of the statue had advanced degrees and held responsible jobs. Our academic and professional achievements are really an unconscious way of justifying our existence and of honoring those who died. When we gathered at the Women's Memorial in 1993, we were all consoled and strengthened by sharing some of our sad memories and finding comfort through being together. We never totally get over trauma, but we can learn from it and move forward, and, with support, lead a good and productive life.

Saying Goodbye to Jerry

It was not until the dedication of the Women's Memorial in 1993 that my overwhelming sadness at Jerry's loss finally poured out. Over the years, Joan had realized how much I cared for this helicopter pilot who rescued the injured, who always understood me. Joan often came with me on visits to the Wall, where I would lay a single yellow rose below the place where his name was listed as Missing in Action. While doing this, I often thought of the yellow ribbons that have sprouted in subsequent wars, symbols that mean "Bring them home safe."

In 1993, after the dedication ceremonies at the women's statue had ended, I walked over to the Vietnam Veterans Memorial to visit names of friends and former loved ones listed on the Wall. This time, when I got to Jerry's name, beside the yellow rose I left a love letter—my only one ever—saying goodbye. After many years of hoping, I decided to change Jerry's status in my memory from MIA to KIA (Killed in Action). I was sad but told myself I was facing reality, ending a chapter of my life that had been left unfinished. Perhaps I could finally get closure. Declaring Jerry KIA meant I no longer considered his status ambiguous.

Many years later, I typed Jerry's name into a computer search. I did not hold my breath. I wasn't sure if I wanted a definitive answer and honestly thought nothing would show up. I was wrong. I learned that there had been sightings of Jerry and his crew in 1994. The US military acknowledged the possibility of their survival. The chopper wreckage had been discovered. It showed the helicopter had had mechanical problems and had been blown out of the sky, yet it was intact when it landed. The men could have survived and probably would have been captured in that enemy stronghold. No one knows whether any of the crew members are still alive, but chances seem good.

Realizing this now, I feel so guilty. Not for loving him. Not because he was married. Not because I have a husband and son I love. Not because of secrets of the heart. Not for any of these reasons.

I feel guilty because I declared him dead in my thoughts.

Twentieth Anniversary of the Vietnam Women's Memorial

In 2013, I volunteered to be one of the speakers at

the twentieth anniversary of the Women's Memorial. I had come a long way from the days when I did not often share my feelings or my status as a veteran. I now believe that it is important for everyone, not just fellow veterans, to understand what women have been through in war.

After I finished my talk at the Women's Memorial, my nurse veteran friends, some in tears, hugged me. Then we decided to walk over to the Wall. In the past, every time I visited the Wall, I left a yellow flower there in memory of Colonel Graham. But this time I had no flower to leave.

I had arrived in Washington a few days earlier. Over the weekend, I went to a number of florist shops, but none were open. After speaking about this with the concierge at my hotel, I took the Metro to another hotel, which he assured me had a flower shop. The shop was closed.

Walking over to the Wall after the anniversary ceremony for the Women's Memorial, I felt so sad. This would be the first time I had no flower for Colonel Graham. As we were walking along the Wall looking at all the names, a boy in a Cub Scout uniform came up to me and handed me a single yellow rose. My friends gasped as I took it and, in tears, thanked my young benefactor. We all hugged, understanding this was more than a mere coincidence. I held the rose close and thought of Colonel Graham. By giving me this flower, the Scout did what Colonel Graham had done for me so many years ago. I placed the rose below her name on the Wall and silently thanked her, again.

SUSAN HUNT BABINSKI

Acknowledgments

Hubert F. Babinski

SUSAN, MY WIFE of forty-eight years, was still working on this memoir when she died on July 14, 2018. She very much wanted to publish this book but did not live long enough to complete it. I had always encouraged her work on the Vietnam memoir, but I did not read any of it until after she died. It was clear to me from before our marriage in 1970 that Vietnam was her territory. I never went with her on any of the anti-war marches or Veterans Day ceremonies she attended.

After she died, I collected all the different drafts of her memoir in progress. She had been working on this project off and on for decades. I read through everything carefully and eventually organized her stories chronologically to give a picture of her year in Vietnam from 1967 to 1968.

In January 2023, I shared the edited manuscript with Rebecca Mlynarczyk, a member of Susan's writing group, which met monthly for many years. Rebecca knew the book had promise and sent it to the founders of Purple Breeze Press—Frances Ward, President; Norbert Elliot, Acquisitions Editor; and Meg Vezzu, Designer and Copy Editor. Feeling that this was a compelling and important story of a woman's experience in war, they offered me a contract within days, which I was glad to sign. Work on the book progressed very quickly after that.

There are many people to thank for making this dream a reality: the team at Purple Breeze Press for their care and professionalism in publishing Susan's book; Pat Juell and Jane Isenberg, members of Susan's writing group, for reading and responding to previous drafts; Diane Carlson Evans, for her tireless work through the Vietnam Women's Memorial Foundation to honor the contributions of women who served there; Ruthie Roberts, for invaluable help during the publication process; Carl Burton, for assistance in locating and selecting photographs from Susan's year in Vietnam; Mindy Lewis, for her help in contacting reviewers; Mel Oldenburg, for supporting me in so many ways; and our son, Andrzej Babinski, for help with technology and everything else.

I especially want to thank Rebecca. During the process of bringing Susan's book to press, she served as a developmental editor, bringing the book together in ways that only a fellow writer could. Rebecca took on securing advanced praise for the book from those most knowledgeable about Susan's contributions, and she collaborated with the press on each stage of the publication process, from selecting the photos to designing the book. It is lovely to think of the connection between Susan and Rebecca, now embodied by this book.

To all these people and many more I owe an immense debt of gratitude.

Fifty-five years after Susan stepped onto a Braniff Airlines plane in Saigon to fly home from her tour in Vietnam, her desire to publish a book about the year that changed her life has finally been realized. Not only is this book a moving personal memoir. It is also a valuable piece of United States history, just one account of the effects the Vietnam War had on the women and men who lived and sometimes died there.

February 15, 2023
New York, New York

SUSAN HUNT BABINSKI

Made in United States
North Haven, CT
04 January 2024